Fishing
THE
Big Four

MILT ROSKO

BURFORD BOOKS

Printed in the United States of America.

10 9 8 7 6 5 4 3 2 1

Library of Congress Cataloging-in- Publication Data
Rosko, Milt.
    Fishing the big four: a guide for saltwater anglers/ Milt Rosko.
        p. cm.
    ISBN 1-58080-091-2
        1. Saltwater fishing. I. Title.

SH457 .R673 2001
799.1`6—dc21

                                                          2001043218

Fishing
THE
Big Four

By the same author

Secrets of Striped Bass Fishing

Fishing from Boats

Spin-Fishing: The System That Does It All

The Complete Book of Saltwater Fishing

Dedication

We dedicate this book to the many

warm friends we have met and enjoyed

fishing with along the seacoast

Claude Bain unhooks a Chesapeake Bay striper landed off Virginia Beach by Robin Magrisi while trolling.

CONTENTS

Stuart Newman hooked the big bluefish being unhooked by Capt. Tony DiLernia of "Rocket Charters" while casting a popping plug. Spinning tackle and surface plugs result in exciting surface action.

ACKNOWLEDGMENTS

It's quite proper for an author to acknowledge those individuals who have contributed to the book. Writing a book such as this is a difficult task. As you can appreciate, it was my dad who introduced me to this lifelong passion. Not only did I learn from him, but I also enjoyed his companionship.

As to writing, the first person to come to mind was the late Frank Woolner, editor of *Salt Water Sportsman,* who published the first article I wrote way back in 1953. There were others, too, including Miss Rizzolo, my English teacher at West Side High School in Newark, New Jersey, and Miss Carpenter, my typing teacher at the time. The skills they taught me have endured and helped me in every facet of my life.

The people who helped me on the angling front include Charlie Searles, the noted Realtor from Rahway and one of the finest jetty jockeys of all time, who always caught stripers even when no one else did. There was the late Captain Frank Cline of the party boat *Rambler,* who shared many tips in catching that "funny-looking" fish, the fluke. When it came to bluefish, there was the late Captain Otto Reut with his *First Timer,* a familiar fixture at Sandy Hook. And there was the late Johnny Sciortino, of Johnny's Landing fame, from whose rental rowboats (yes, that was when oar power got you there!) I caught many a weakfish.

Were I to continue, the list would number into the thousands. Believe me, no one writes a book such as this without tips gleaned from others. Toward that end, I have been very fortunate in that I always made it a point to team up with the finest anglers, and often learned more in a single day or night of fishing than I would have learned in a season of trial and error on my own.

It is with great respect that I acknowledge and thank all these people for the help they offered, which resulted in my days along the seacoast being among the most enjoyable of my life. For this I am eternally grateful and extend my heartfelt thanks.

Special thanks to Jennifer Basilio, my granddaughter, who not only fishes with me but also contributed the line drawings of various rigs throughout this book. Her attention to detail demonstrates a talent certain to enhance her graphic design career. Alan Sherman's first work to achieve national book exposure appeared in my *Complete Book of Saltwater Fishing.* His fine line drawings of the lures herein are a testament to his talents.

There's the lady in my life, too. She deserves my gratitude for so much. June and I were classmates in junior high school, and from that beginning have enjoyed a lifetime together. Borrowing her mom's car, we visited the seacoast often. It didn't take her long to score with fluke, weakfish, and blues. It was on the Sea Bright rock wall using an Ed's 8 block tin squid that she landed a 7-pound striper, her first. The date was June 13, 1951, and it completed her favorite four—all while we were still dating, more than 50 years ago. She's not only fished with me in some of the world's most exotic fishing spots, she's prepared countless fine seafood dinners, and shares many of the recipes in this book. Her camera handling is superb, and whenever I'm in the picture—and in many other photos as well—the credit rightfully belongs to her.

Milt Rosko

It was an exciting morning for me, a seven-year-old accompanying his dad on a fishing excursion out of Shark River Inlet on the central New Jersey coast. The all-day party boats had sailed, and Captain Bert's charter boat was sitting at dockside. Lucky for us, he put together the makeup charter that included dad and me.

Just being on a boat and on the broad expanse of the ocean was excitement in itself. Dad rigged me up with a stiff split-bamboo rod and a knucklebuster reel loaded with Cuttyhunk linen line, baiting my bottom rig with a strip of squid.

Just a short distance from shore, north of the inlet, the captain shut down the engine and the six of us permitted our rigs to settle into the depths. I remember to this day the handle of the knucklebuster reel spinning backward as the sinker pulled the rig to the bottom.

Not more than five minutes passed before the rod of an angler alongside me arched over, and soon he swung aboard his catch. I really don't remember what it was, for suddenly my rod was pulled down hard to the gunwale, which was chest-high for me. It provided support as I reeled for what seemed like an eternity, until Dad assisted me in swinging a 1 1/2-pound weakfish aboard. Its pretty purple, yellow, white, and golden hues glistened in the morning sun. I don't know who was prouder, Dad or me.

It was not only my first fish; it was the beginning of a love affair with what I've come to call my favorite four.

Soon rods were bending all around the cockpit as other weakfish came aboard. I was soon to add another fish to my catch, a funny-looking fish. It was flat, with a brown top and white bottom. I'd landed number two of my favorite four, a fat, 2-pound beauty that everybody called a fluke, more properly known as summer flounder.

It was later that summer while fishing from a pier in Keansburg that I landed my first bluefish, number three of the favorite four. It was a "snapper" blue, measuring about 7 inches in length. A bamboo pole, length of line, cork float, and spearing-baited hook were the undoing of this one, along with several others that Dad and I landed.

Fast-forward nine years to May 16, 1946. I was casting with my first split-bamboo surf rod and a Penn Surfmaster reel with a free-spool mechanism; no more knucklebusters for me. I fished from the rocks adjacent to the bridge spanning the Shrewsbury River at Highlands,

New Jersey. Using as bait a tapeworm fished on the bottom, I realized the fish of my dreams, a 6 1/2-pound striped bass. This exciting accomplishment marked my final species of the favorite four.

Today I enjoy catching the favorite four as much as I did catching each of them for the first time. They're still the favorite four of both my wife, June, and me as we travel along all three coasts and to exotic destinations. We've caught them from Maine to Louisiana, and stripers off the Golden Gate, and enjoyed every minute of it. It's without question that we've enjoyed them at the table, too, prepared many ways.

That's the reason I wrote this book. It's to tell you how you, too, can enjoy fishing for and catching striped bass, bluefish, weakfish, and fluke. Yes, they're fun to catch and great to eat, making for a combination that just can't be beat. Importantly, fishing for all four can be the most contemplative of pastimes. This is fishing as it should be, relaxing, fun for the entire family, with some fish for the table, and others returned to the water for another day.

Throughout this book I've attempted to cover every technique and method that I've employed over a span of many years. I've tried to remember them all. Rest assured that whether you're a newcomer or veteran angler, you'll enhance your enjoyment by absorbing what's between this book's covers. The use of a teaser when casting or jigging from boat or shore, and the use of a breeches buoy rig with live bait, are just a couple of tips that would enhance the enjoyment of thousands of anglers were they to just take the time to try them. There are scores of other tips, too.

I wanted this book to be organized in a manner that would make for ease of reading, yet be functional as a reference. So you'll first be introduced to each of the four species, the striped bass, bluefish, weakfish, and fluke. These early chapters won't help you catch fish, but you'll have a better understanding of each species.

There's such a great difference in tackle and techniques from boats and shore that I elected to separate the two. From boat or shore, though, you'll find an in-depth discussion of the most popular methods, down to the minutest details to enhance your enjoyment and improve your catch. Because fly fishing is done both from beach and boat, and is in itself such a unique science, it's covered in a chapter of its own.

While catching the favorite four is truly enjoyable, I felt it important to devote chapters to the care of these fine table fish. All too often a catch isn't properly cared for or cleaned, which detracts from its flavor and freshness by the time it reaches the kitchen. It's in the kitchen that our favorite four may be transformed into a delicious meal. My wife, June, provides her favorite recipes for all four species, guaranteed to please the most discriminating taste.

On occasion I'll land a Northeast Super Grand Slam: all four species on the same day. It's the pinnacle of the love affair that began a long time ago and continues strong. I invite you to join me in pursuing this rewarding passion, with striped bass, bluefish, weakfish, and fluke being the ultimate reward.

Bluefish like this beauty landed by the author will readily strike a surface swimming plug retrieved slowly.

I
Meet the Big Four

Within sight of famous Montauk Light, both boat and beach anglers enjoy exciting fishing for striped bass, bluefish, weakfish, and fluke.

1

STRIPED BASS

The striped bass, *Morone saxatilis,* is unquestionably one of America's favorite game and food fish. It is found in greatest abundance throughout the Northeast, from the Chesapeake Bay to Maine. Local populations travel north to Canada's Maritime Provinces, and to the south they're found in Florida's St. John's River.

Along the Gulf of Mexico small populations have established residence in rivers of western Florida, Alabama, Louisiana, and Texas. These particular populations seldom venture far from their native rivers and tributaries.

The striped bass was introduced on the Pacific coast in 1886 from stocks of fish netted in New Jersey's Navesink River. From that small beginning the population flourished. It now represents a formidable fishery in the greater San Francisco Bay area. Over a span of years some of the Pacific striped bass have extended their range from as far south as Los Angeles to the Columbia River in Washington.

Striper Habits and Habitat

Striped bass are anadromous, moving from ocean, sound, and bay waters and ascending coastal rivers to spawn. Some populations, such as New York's Hudson River fish, move very short distances through their lifetime. They often spend spring through fall in the broad reaches of Long Island Sound, then return to spend the winter dormant in the Hudson's upper reaches. Much the same is true of the Delaware River population, which returns to its birthplace to spend the winter. Spawning takes place in spring, and the cycle is repeated.

Other populations spawn in the river systems of the Chesapeake and the many broad reaches of the sounds and rivers behind the barrier islands off the Carolinas. Many of these striped bass spend summer and fall off New England, returning to the waters they call home to spawn.

Much the same holds true on the Pacific coast, where the majority of striped bass return to the fresh and brackish water of the Sacramento–San Joaquin Delta to spend the winter, after which they spawn in spring. As the waters warm they spread out, returning to their favorite haunts in the San Francisco Bay and adjacent waterways.

There are also populations of striped bass that are landlocked. When damming rivers created an impoundment, such as Lakes Marion and Moultrie in South Carolina, the native populations of those rivers were trapped. Surprisingly, they have continued to propagate, despite not returning to the ocean. The same holds true for those striped bass found in the Kerr Reservoir in North Carolina. Both locations provide excellent fishing, using much the same techniques employed in all the areas where striped bass are found. Many of these landlocked stripers grow to the same respectable size as their ocean-traveling cousins. This is a result of the tremendous amount of forage, primarily herring and shad, found in the impoundments.

Still another impoundment in the southwest is Lake Texoma, a flood-control project on the border of Texas and Oklahoma that's predominantly fresh water, with tributary rivers such as the Red River and Washita River, both of which have a high saline content. Striped bass were introduced to these waters in the 1960s, transplanted from Lakes Marion and Moultrie in South Carolina, and they've adapted extremely well. Texoma has enjoyed natural spawning for many years, and the population has flourished. Indeed, striped bass have moved into every major tributary of the Red River all the way to the Gulf of Mexico.

Population Changes and Conservation

In the past half century all the various populations of striped bass have undergone periods of plenty and periods of scarcity. Some of the fluctuations are natural phenomena, where ideal spawning conditions in spring provide a sizable new population of juveniles. Several years of poor conditions, brought about by natural and man-made pollutants, result in severely depleted spawning opportunities and few young stripers entering the fishery.

Excessive harvest, by both commercial and sport fishermen, contributed to a severe decline of striped bass populations not long ago. This severe decline resulted in a period during the 1980s when opportunities to regularly catch striped bass were limited.

The International Game Fish Association maintains world-record catches in 20 different line classes, ranging from 2-pound test through

80-pound test. It's interesting to note that 15 of the 20 record catches were taken during the period from 1971 through 1987, and most weighed 56 pounds or more, with several in the 60- to 70-pound class. The current all-tackle record weighed 78 pounds, 8 ounces and was landed September 21, 1982, by Albert R. McReynolds while fishing off Atlantic City, New Jersey.

Catches of big striped bass during that era, especially those in the 45- to 55-pound class, were quite common. The excesses from both commercial and sport fishermen eventually decimated the population, and today it's a rare occurrence when fish weighing 50 pounds or more are landed. However, scientists feel that the dominant year classes currently in the 25- to 35-pound range will begin to reach record-breaking weights within the next five to seven years.

As a result of prudent management of the striped bass fishery by both federal and state agencies throughout the range of this fine game fish, the population has rebounded, and as this book is written is at a healthier level than in many years.

Still, care must be exercised by both commercial and recreational fishermen to ensure that reasonable quantities of these fine fish are caught, as opposed to exploiting the fishery as was done in the past.

All too often the emphasis, even with regulations in place, is on killing as many fish, and especially the breeders, as is permitted by law. Recreational anglers would do well to catch their limit, but limit their kill to what is needed for the table. Release big fish in particular, because these are the spawning bass that propagate future generations.

As a case in point, scientists have determined that female striped bass measuring 20 to 24 inches in length are approximately five years old and produce 50,000 to 60,000 eggs. An older striped bass, 11 to 12 years old and weighing 35 pounds, may produce upward of 5 million eggs. You can easily appreciate that to ensure a sustainable fishery, it's far better to harvest more of the smaller fish for the table—and these are the finest table-quality fish anyway—as opposed to depleting the older stock.

Keep in mind that it takes 100 5-year-old stripers to produce the eggs of a single 35-pound 12-year-old. Although recreational anglers certainly like to land a trophy fish, a single trophy-sized striped bass is certainly more than adequate; return others to ensure the population's stability.

As this book is being written, the majority of striped bass caught by recreational anglers range from 4 to 20 pounds, making them ideally suited to light-tackle fishing, whether from a boat or from the beach.

There was a time when it was common to encounter fish in the 40- to 50-pound class, but that class of fish has been severely depleted, and it will take several more years for the bigger fish to regain their dominance.

Feeding Habits

The striped bass has gained a reputation as "the prince of the unpredictables." Rightly so, for while many species of ocean fish travel and feed with a degree of predictability, this is not so with the striped bass. Each time you feel you've mastered the techniques for catching this fine game fish, the princely striper changes its pattern of movements or feeding habits. More often the change of pattern is the result of the availability of forage. Striped bass are schooling fish, so there must be a substantial availability of forage in the waters where they take up residence. Often, as forage moves from an area—as is the case with schools of menhaden, mackerel, herring, and sand eels—the bass follow along, always eager to have an easy meal readily available.

While striped bass spend much of their life in the ocean, they're basically inshore feeders. There are rare occasions when they're caught several miles from shore, but for the most part they range along the surf line. They're also found on rocky bottoms and along the lumps and ridges close to shore, usually within 3 miles of the beach, where food is readily available.

The striper readily adapts to changing food supplies. Forage species often go through cycles where great abundance is followed by periods of scarcity. Thus, while feeding extensively on menhaden, the bass are quick to adjust and enjoy meals of mackerel or herring should menhaden not be available.

The striper is an opportunist, often feeding on a wide variety in a single day. The stomach contents of striped bass I've caught over many years have included flounder, weakfish, bluefish, squid, blue crabs, calico crabs, rock crabs, shrimp, sand bugs, eels, shad, mullet, several species of seaworm, clams, and mussels. Undoubtedly there were more species that I couldn't identify.

Striped Bass and the Angler

Stripers' inshore availability has made them particularly popular with anglers who fish from small boats, for with their craft they can fish the open reaches of the ocean, the nearby sound and river waters, and even the estuaries, with ease.

Shore-based anglers fish from the sand beaches or rock jetties and groins, from bridges spanning rivers, and from the many docks and

A selection of saltwater flies guaranteed to bring strikes from all of the species discussed in this book.

piers that extend into rivers and bays. There's hardly a waterway in their range that doesn't support a resident population of stripers during spring, summer, and fall. Many of the fish return to the same waters year after year following a winter of hibernation in their home waters.

Devotees of the striped bass, more than any other species, are a dedicated clan that worship at the shrine of this princely game fish. Stripers represent the same lifelong challenge to saltwater fishermen that trout do to freshwater anglers. They're a challenge that demands mastering a variety of skills and adapting to the ever-changing habits of this ocean traveler.

Perhaps this is because the striper is available under such a wide variety of conditions, in varied waterways, and may be sought using a wide array of tackle. Whatever the case, take care before you target them, for once you've added stripers to your list of achievements, you may find that ultimately you're the one hooked by a lifetime challenge.

Striped Bass on the Table

When properly caught, cleaned, and prepared for the table, the striped bass is a gourmet's delight. Its white, mild-flavored meat may be prepared using a wide range of recipes.

Because the meat is mild and firm, it freezes well. Many anglers are not averse to stocking their freezer for the winter. Toward this end it is generally agreed that the smaller striped bass, from 4 to 10 pounds (check state regulations to ensure compliance on the size of striped bass you keep) are more desirable than the big spawners, a good reason to release the heavyweights.

By now you've hopefully learned enough about striped bass to pique your interest. In subsequent chapters there will be detailed discussion of the tackle, lures, baits, and techniques needed to catch this great game fish.

Jim Stabile used a light spinning outfit to subdue this school striper while fishing in sight of the New York skyline.

2

BLUEFISH

The bluefish, *Pomatomus saltatrix,* is a world traveler found in almost all of the temperate oceans. It is also one of the most vicious game fish anglers encounter. Known for its formidable, very sharp teeth, it has a reputation for wildly attacking schools of forage fish such as menhaden, mackerel, and herring. It indiscriminately bites huge chunks from the fish, sometimes cutting them completely in half then quickly circling back to pick up the pieces. Often it will feed, regurgitate what it has consumed, and begin feeding again.

The Fish and Its Habits

There is no set migration pattern; some schools of bluefish move north and south along the Atlantic coast, while others move from west to east. The general pattern of movement is from Florida and the Carolinas northward in spring, with a westerly movement of fish that have wintered in offshore waters. Some travel as far north as Canada's Maritime Provinces during early spring, retreating to southern climes as the late-autumn storms buffet the coast.

Bluefish generally spawn in early summer, some in coastal bays, others in the broad reaches of the ocean. The young bluefish grow rapidly, attaining 8 to 10 inches in length by late summer and early autumn, when they invade coastal rivers, bays, and estuaries. Fish of the year are called snappers and provide excellent sport for youngsters who fish for them from docks, piers, bridges, and bulkheads in protected waterways. These same fish will return the following spring, having attained a size of 12 to 15 inches (now nicknamed tailors), and spend much of their time in protected coastal waters and along the surf, where they provide fine sport and are of a size that is preferred for the table.

Atlantic coast anglers often encounter bluefish of varying sizes, with schools generally composed of same-sized fish, although there are occasions where bluefish of many sizes mix together. The largest bluefish, those ranging from 15 to 20 pounds or more, are called alligators for their huge, sharp teeth. It's not unusual for numerous bluefish in the 20-pound class to be caught each season throughout their entire range. Catches beyond that weight are rare occurrences.

The world-record bluefish as recognized by the International Game Fish Association weighed 31 pounds, 12 ounces and was caught off Hatteras, North Carolina, on January 30, 1972, by James M. Hussey. Interesting to note is that very few of the 20 different line-class records exceed 20 pounds.

Occasional bluefish are caught along the Atlantic coast that range from 25 to 30 pounds, but these are the exception.

Caution is the byword of bluefish anglers, for even the tiniest snapper can inflict cuts and bites if you're not careful while handling it. Bigger fish can inflict serious injury in an instant.

In recent years the bluefish population reached peak levels along the Atlantic coast. Anglers must count their blessings for this period of abundance, because bluefish are cyclical, with years of plenty followed by periods when they simply disappear from the coastal scene. Little is known about what causes such major swings in the populations.

Bluefish schools often number in the thousands. When feeding on the surface they sometimes churn the water to a froth as acres upon acres of feeding fish attack forage. Electronic fishfinders often disclose

Anglers aboard the party boat *Lazybones* diamond-jig for big bluefish at Shagwong Reef, at the easternmost tip of Long Island, New York.

tightly packed fish from the surface to the bottom all ravenously feeding. Because huge quantities of forage are necessary to support a population of bluefish, their movements generally follow the food supply.

It's doubtful there's anything that lives in the ocean that bluefish won't eat, including their own! Staples in their diet include menhaden, mackerel, herring, mullet, spearing, sand eels, and the young of many game and food fish. They'll also feed on clams when storms tumble them about and break open their shells, or on any variety of crabs, sand bugs, seaworms, shrimp, and squid.

Although bluefish are occasionally encountered along the edge of the continental shelf as they migrate, for the most part they're inshore residents. They set up residence well within range of anglers who seek them from small boats, charter rigs, and party packets.

Bluefish and the Angler

Anglers who fish from boats employ a variety of techniques to catch bluefish, including trolling, chumming, bottom fishing, jigging, casting, and fly fishing. Schools of bluefish generally set up residence in a particular area where food is plentiful, particularly on lumps and ridges and along rip lines where currents clash and baitfish are trapped. It's not unusual for a population to stay in one area for the entire summer season, rarely moving so long as the food supply is plentiful.

Casters who fish from beach, jetty, or groin, and from coastal docks, piers, and bulkheads, are almost at the whim of the fish's movements. The bluefish caught by casters are most often opportunists that will literally herd schools of baitfish. It's not unusual for a school of bluefish to trap a school of menhaden, mullet, or other forage along the beach and pursue it for many miles. If you're fortunate enough to be on the scene you enjoy bonanza fishing, often having to travel along the beach, following the movements of the slashing bluefish, often hooking a fish on almost every cast.

Bluefish are spectacular fighters and strike a wide variety of lures. Unquestionably the most exciting action is when the blues are feeding on the surface. Their surface feeding is often accompanied by huge numbers of seagulls, all screaming and diving to pick up the pieces of forage that have been chopped to pieces by the blues. At this time the blues will readily strike a surface plug such as a swimmer, popper, or darter. In so doing they'll often leap into the air repeatedly, testing an angler and his tackle to the limit.

There are occasions when shore-based casters will observe nary a sign of bluefish, particularly when they're feeding on sand lance, popularly called sand eels. The long, thin silvery and brown baitfish, unlike most species that travel to the surface and leap into the air to avoid the teeth of the blues, instead dive into the depths, often burrowing into the sand to escape the blues. At such times their activity isn't noticed. Leadhead jigs and stainless-steel jigs that probe the depths when cast from beach and rock pile often provide sterling action.

Casters who know the water they plan to fish often seek out deep holes between offshore bars, or deep sluices inside the surf's bar formations. It's here that bluefish will often move in, knowing there's a

This big bluefish struck a leadhead jig with a plastic tail as the party boat *Gambler* drifted off Manasquan Inlet, New Jersey.

A chunk bait consisting of the head of a menhaden proves effective for bluefish.

supply of food awaiting them. The same holds true at points of land, where tidal flow causes rips and currents in which baitfish are often trapped. These areas are often fished with chunk baits on the bottom. It then becomes a waiting game, with lightning-fast action once the prowling bluefish move in.

Bluefish on the Table

Bluefish, particularly those ranging in weight from 1 to 6 pounds, are delicious and may be prepared in a variety of ways. It is, however, extremely important that bluefish be properly cared for when caught. Their digestive systems are such that the huge quantity of food often found in their stomach continues to break down, and this will quickly compromise the quality of the fish without proper handling. Bleeding the fish immediately is paramount, as is removal of the stomach and its contents, after which the fish should be washed with salt water and immediately iced. I'll describe final cleaning in a later chapter.

The delicate flavor of bluefish is enhanced with proper preparation. It's extremely important that bluefish not be overcooked; this causes the fish to become dry and take on a heavy flavor. Many veteran cooks test the texture of the fish every few minutes while cooking. As soon as the bluefish meat begins to flake it's ready to be served.

Given the depletion of tuna in offshore waters, many coastal anglers who formerly sought them now concentrate their efforts on bluefish.

This places a lot of pressure on the stocks. Thus, it's wise to save only the quantity of fish you plan to immediately use for the table, releasing the balance to ensure quality fishing in the future. Bluefish, because of their soft flesh, do not freeze well, and it just doesn't make sense to kill a limit of the big blues.

Through the remaining chapters, whether you fish from shore or boat, you'll experience firsthand the kind of tackle best suited to catching bluefish, along with the lures, baits, and techniques to enhance your score with this vicious game fish.

Few will question the tenacity of the bluefish. It certainly is the toughest fighting of the favorite four I discuss in this book. It will challenge you and your skills and tackle to the utmost. At times it viciously attacks whatever you present, while on other occasions it rejects your best-placed offerings. You'll find it rewarding to seek this blue battler with its sharp teeth and ornery disposition.

Bluefish have extremely sharp teeth and you should always be careful while unhooking them, as the teeth can inflict serious injury.

3

WEAKFISH

The weakfish, *Cynoscion regalis,* and its close cousin the spotted sea trout, *C. nebulosus,* are found in the inshore reaches of both the Atlantic Ocean and Gulf of Mexico. Although this book deals primarily with seeking out and catching weakfish, the techniques apply equally to the spotted sea trout. In fact, there's a great deal of overlap in their ranges. In general terms the weakfish is in greatest supply from the Carolinas north, and the spotted sea trout from the Carolinas to Texas.

The weakfish derives its name from the fact it has a very thin mouth structure. Once you hook a weakfish you must take great care in landing it. With too much drag pressure, or if you attempt to lift the fish while landing, the hook will often rip from its mouth.

It's a very pretty fish, with coloration on its back that includes olive, blue, lavender, with a blush of gold and copper. Its pronounced yellow fins have earned it the nickname yellowfin. The weakfish also has very sharp, needlelike teeth. The profile of the spotted sea trout is identical, with the exception that its coloration is enhanced with a series of black dots, or spots, on its back, dorsal fin, and tail.

Weakfish Diet and Habitat

These fish are inshore residents that populate almost every estuary, river, bay, or sound in their range. They're also found in the open ocean, particularly when they migrate. Wintering off the Virginia and Carolina coast, weakfish begin their trek north and west in early spring and stay through late fall, when the first fall nor'easter and a drop in water temperature send them to climes more to their liking.

Both the weakfish and spotted sea trout move in from open ocean and gulf waters in spring, where they take up residence in coastal bays and sounds to tend to their spawning chores. They then spend the summer feeding aggressively, adding weight from the plentiful supply of food in the protected inshore waterways. While the population is usually spread over a wide area in summer, as the waters begin to cool in autumn the weakfish begin to congregate in huge schools, moving into ocean waters by the thousands to begin their trek south to their wintering grounds.

Weakfish aren't fussy when it comes to what they'll eat. They're opportunists, feeding on small forage such as sand eels, mullet, killies, spearing, rainfish, and menhaden. They also feed on the fry of almost any fish, including bluefish, stripers, and fluke, and even their own.

Throughout the weakfish's range the common grass shrimp is plentiful and constitutes a sizable portion of its diet. To the south they also feed on larger, market-sized shrimp, as do spotted sea trout. They also feed extensively on almost any small crabs, clams broken open and

The author landed this tiderunner weakfish while casting a rattle plug in the swift waters of New Jersey's Manasquan River.

exposed by coastal storms, squid, sand bugs, and any of the many varieties of seaworm.

Weakfish move a great deal during the course of a day. They'll take up stations along tide rips and eddies to gorge on food swept their way. But stemming the tide takes energy, and when the currents become too swift they'll fan out to the quiet waters of tidal bays and estuaries, moving along the sod banks and marsh grass. Here they find a plentiful supply of forage species and an ever-present and unlimited quantity of their favorite, the grass shrimp.

Conservation

Weakfish are cyclical, as are striped bass and bluefish, with periods of plenty followed by years when but limited numbers are encountered. Some of the cyclical swings have been attributed to natural circumstances, such as periods of ideal spawning conditions followed by periods with but limited spawning results. Some of the decline has also been attributed to pollution, but increased concern for clean waterways has all but eliminated this problem.

A review of the 20 line-class world records indicates that the last time a record was broken was in 1990, with all the other records posted in the 1980s. As with striped bass, excessive fishing by both sport and commercial interests in that era depleted the populations drastically. It is anticipated that the current resurgence of weakfish will result in limited numbers reaching world-record size in the next four to six years. The current world-record weakfish is a tie. On October 11, 1984, Dennis Roger Rooney landed a 19-pound, 2-ounce specimen while fishing Jones Beach Inlet in Long Island, New York. Another fish of the same size was caught on May 20, 1989, by William E. Thomas, who fished in Delaware Bay, New Jersey.

The spotted sea trout does not grow as large as the weakfish, but it comes close. The current all-tackle world record is held by Craig F. Carson, who landed a 17-pound, 7-ounce beauty on May 11, 1995, while fishing out of Fort Pierce, Florida.

The spotted sea trout hasn't fared as well as the weakfish; it continues to be plagued by pollution along the Mississippi delta. This is a direct result of agricultural, commercial, and industrial pollutants traveling the entire length of the Mississippi and spreading oxygen-consuming nutrients throughout the inshore Gulf of Mexico.

The fine eating quality of these species contributed to their decline as well, because there's always a ready market. This often resulted in extensive commercial netting when the weakfish and spotted sea trout were schooled up and dormant during winter. Regulation of both the commercial and recreational fisheries in recent years has resulted in a remarkable comeback of the weakfish, and to a lesser degree the spotted sea trout as well.

As a general rule the quantity of smaller fish exceeds that of larger specimens. Huge schools of 8- to 12-inch fish often invade coastal bays and rivers, and most states now protect fish of this size, which helps build the population. Especially encouraging in recent years is the gradual increase in the size of each year class of weakfish. Thus anglers have an opportunity to catch fish from legal size (depending on each state's regulations) on up to tiderunner size—weakfish that exceed the 10-pound mark—with a good mix of all sizes in between.

It's not unusual to encounter sizable schools of weakfish. It's also not unusual to get caught up in the excitement of catching them, and keeping more than you really need. Always make a point remembering the days when this popular species almost disappeared from the coastal scene. As such it's wise to limit your catch, carefully practicing catch-and-release to ensure the continued abundance of this "trout" of the saltwater angler.

Weakfish and the Angler

Anglers who seek weakfish from boats consider them a light-tackle challenge, with light spinning and casting tackle rated for 10- to 12-pound-test line ideal. They also provide fine casting opportunities for

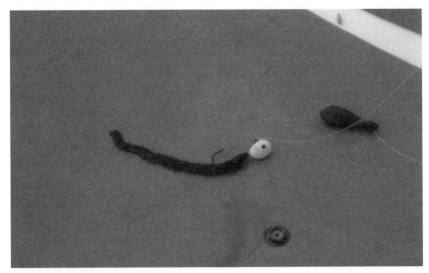

The floating jighead with a live sandworm bait is a favorite of anglers who fish the Indian River in Delaware.

boat anglers who prefer fly fishing. Depending on the areas fished, boatmen employ a variety of techniques, including casting, trolling, chumming, bottom fishing, and casting and jigging artificials.

Shore-based anglers also post many good scores, for weakfish regularly frequent the surf and the waters surrounding coastal jetties and groins. They particularly like to take up residence in the tidal currents around docks, piers, and bridges. At night they can often be seen stemming the tide along the shadow line of the lights from these structures. They wait for the current to sweep a crab, shrimp, or small fish their way, whereupon they move up to engulf it, quickly returning to their stations on the shadow line.

When they're in the shallows, weakfish provide exciting opportunities for the fly caster. Although they'll take a surface popper or slider worked along marsh grass, they're especially responsive to a Clouser or Deceiver worked on a sinking line in the thin water extending out from the shoreline.

As a general rule the weakfish is most responsive to small lures. Small flies just an inch in length and 1/8-ounce leadheads with 3-inch plastic tails or subsurface swimming plugs of the same size will result in more strikes than the larger lures you'd most often be using for striped bass and bluefish. The weakfish is a patient feeder; examination of stomach contents will often reveal literally hundreds of grass shrimp and tiny fry, inhaled as they move along the shallows to feed.

Weakfish on the Table

Weakfish are fine table fish, but great care must be taken to properly care for them: They have softer, more delicate flesh than striped bass or fluke. Ice is the key once they're landed. Many anglers gut their weakfish, and then let them rest on ice for several hours, permitting the flesh to firm up and making filleting easier. After cleaning they may be frozen, and hold quite well, especially when vacuum packed. As with stripers and bluefish, removal of the dark meat of the lateral line ensures a mild flavor.

As you move to each succeeding chapter, whether you plan to fish from boat or shore, you'll absorb all the details relating to choosing fishing tackle, lures, and baits, and then learn precisely how to catch this prettily hued inshore feeder, the weakfish.

The author used a 9 weight fly rod and sinking line with a Clouser minnow fly to coax a strike from the summer flounder he's unhooking.

4

FLUKE

Brown on the top and white on the bottom, the fluke, properly named summer flounder, *Paralichthys dentatus,* is the most popular inshore bottom feeder found along the Northeast and middle Atlantic coasts.

Throughout this book the fish is referred to as just plain fluke, simply because that's what almost everyone calls it along the seacoast. They're popular because they're fun to catch, at times quite plentiful, but most important, they're among the most delicious table fare the sea has to offer. When filleted, their popular white meat becomes the "fillet of sole" recognized in almost every household.

Types of Flounder

Much as the weakfish has a close cousin in the spotted sea trout, the summer flounder has several cousins that closely resemble it: specifically, the southern flounder *Paralichthys lethostigma* and the gulf flounder *P. albigutta.* Both are smaller in size than fluke, and throughout the Carolinas their ranges overlap. It's not unusual to catch several of each species in the course of a day's fishing. Only on close examination can a distinction be made between species. The primary and easily recognizable difference between the gulf flounder and southern flounder is that the spots on gulf flounder's back are irregular, while they're very distinct and regularly placed on the back of the fluke.

All three of these flatfish are chameleonlike in that the coloration of their brown side changes to blend in with the bottom on which they're dwelling. On a mud or clay bottom, their back takes on an almost black coloration. Over a sand bottom, their back becomes light beige. Over a pebble bottom, the mottled color of their back has distinct markings, not unlike the color and size of the pebbles over which they reside. These flatfish regularly use their fins to bury themselves in the sand or mud bottom, and often only their eyes and back protrude; it takes keen eyesight to distinguish them at this time. When there's a strong storm or a marked drop in water temperature, flatfish will often bury in the sand for days on end, resulting in poor fishing, because they simply don't feed. Only when the temperature and water clarity suit their fancy do they move from the sand to seek a meal, at which time anglers suddenly begin to enjoy good fishing.

All three flounder have mouths filled with sharp teeth, with which they can easily secure any of the many types of live food they encounter as they move along the bottom.

Flounder Habits and Habitat

For the purpose of this book, suffice it to say that the summer flounder, or fluke, is found in greatest abundance from Maine to the Carolinas during late spring, through the summer, and into early autumn. In fall they migrate to the east, wintering along the edge of the continental shelf, returning to the inshore shallows in spring, where they spread out. Some spend the summer in the ocean, on lumps and ridges, or along the surf. Others move into the waters of sounds, bays, rivers, and tidal estuaries.

When a fluke arrives inshore from a winter in shelf waters, it has had to travel more than 100 miles, and it's lean. It's during the summer that it will add thickness to its frame and length to its body before the long trip eastward for the winter.

June Rosko holds aloft a doormat fluke she landed while drifting a strip bait in the shallows reaches of New Jersey's Barnegat Bay.

The southern flounder and gulf flounder take up residence from the Carolinas to Florida, and thence across the gulf coast to Texas, where they spend the entire year inshore along the shallow beaches, often venturing into brackish water, and occasionally into fresh. Both species are small in size, with the southern flounder averaging 1 to 2 pounds in weight, with an occasional 5-pound flatfish, while the gulf flounder is smaller still, seldom weighing more than a pound.

The normal east-to-west migration during spring occurs as inshore waters warm and is usually heralded by the arrival of small fluke, ranging from palm sized to a couple of pounds, followed by the bigger specimens, many of which take up summer residence in ocean and sound waters. It's in the open-water areas where there are lumps, ridges, and rocky outcroppings that a variety of large food is available to them, hence their preference for these waters. Here cunner, sea bass, scup, sand eels, crabs, squid, and other large forage is available. Smaller fluke are content to invade the surf, bays, and rivers where killies, spearing, rainfish, mullet, small crabs, and shrimp satisfy their appetites.

Although bottom feeders, fluke are very aggressive. They move about quickly and cover a wide area as they feed. They move from spot to spot, often taking up residence for weeks or months at a time, depending on the availability of food.

On the offshore grounds, located anywhere from the beach to several miles offshore, you can cover lots of bottom and receive nary a strike. Once you locate a concentration of baitfish atop a lump or ridge, however—which is easily done using electronic fishfinding gear—you'll invariably begin to receive strikes. As with most species, the key to finding fluke is finding where the food is. Every fluke requires a substantial amount of food to sustain it, and it's not averse to moving to find it.

Fluke have a habit of seeking food very close to shore once they take up residence along the beach or in rivers and bays. In the surf and around jetties they're often within fifty feet of where you're standing, feeding in the curl of the breakers, where the waves churn up sand bugs, crabs, sand eels, and other forage.

In bay and river waters they may move into the depths of channels at low tide, but fan out over the flats on the flooding tide. They feed on the plentiful killies, spearing, menhaden, and mullet that frequent the shallows and along the docks, piers, bulkheads, and marsh grass along the perimeter of these waterways. As you develop experience you know just where to fish at various stages of the tide and enjoy great success as a result.

Party boats such as the *Gambler* sail from ports all along the coast, often on a half-day schedule, targeting the plentiful fluke found close to shore.

Fluke and the Angler

Not surprisingly, fluke and their cousins may be taken using much the same methods as for striped bass, weakfish, and bluefish. What is surprising is that although most anglers, out of habit, fish for them on the bottom and drifting with natural baits from boats, by experimenting you'll find that fluke will readily respond to a chum line. They'll also take a trolled or cast swimming plug or jig worked along the bottom.

Shore-based anglers most often bottom fish with natural baits cast from the surf, jetty, pier, or bulkhead, waiting for the fluke to come their way and find their bait. A far better approach is to keep the bait moving, casting and retrieving to cover as much bottom as possible. Still greater enjoyment may result by employing a leadhead jig and teaser combination worked through known haunts of the flatfish.

Conservation

Although fluke are the least glamorous of the favorite four, few serious anglers would pass up a chance of making a nice catch of flatfish. The reason is simple: Not only are they fun to catch and a challenge, but on the dinner table few fish can top them for overall acceptance. Because of this there continues to be substantial fishing pressure on the species from both recreational anglers and commercial fishermen. The species is tightly regulated, and as a result the fishery—which was being greatly depleted in recent years—has stabilized, and continues to provide fine catches. Here too, as I've stated with respect to others of the favorite four, enjoy the sport, but limit your catch to what is reasonable, irrespective of the regulations.

Size

Fluke are the largest of the three flatfish covered herein, and occasional specimens topping 20 pounds have been landed. Many years ago, when large fluke were plentiful, the term *doormat* came into use to identify one that weighed 10 pounds or more. More recently, the title is used to identify those that top the 5-pound mark.

One fluke, or summer flounder as it's called by the International Game Fish Association, that certainly was the size of a doormat was the current world record of 22 pounds, 7 ounces that was landed by Charles Nappi on September 15, 1975, while fishing off Montauk, Long Island, New York.

The current world-record southern flounder was no lightweight, weighing in at a respectable 20 pounds, 9 ounces. It was caught by Larenza W. Mungin on December 23, 1983, while fishing in Nassau Sound, Florida. This was extraordinarily large for this species.

The gulf flounder is much smaller, with the current all-tackle world record weighing in at 6 pounds, 4 ounces. It was caught on November 2, 1996, by Don Davis while fishing off Dauphin Island, Alabama.

Fluke on the Table

Fluke are great when prepared whole, with just the entrails removed and the cavity filled with a seasoned stuffing or crabmeat. Most people prefer to fillet the flatfish, removing a single fillet from the top and bottom of smaller fish, and two fillets each from the top and bottom of larger fish. There are unlimited recipes that may be used to prepare a dinner that will long be remembered.

Because of their firm meat, fluke are excellent when vacuum packed and frozen. They hold for a year or longer in the freezer.

Should the prospect of both catching fluke and enjoying them for dinner arouse your interest, just read on, as subsequent chapters will walk you through each step from tackle selection to lures, baits, and the techniques to catch this "fillet of sole" of the Atlantic.

The advantage of trolling is that once your lines are set you can then cover a great deal of area frequented by stripers.

II
Fishing
FROM Boats

5

TROLLING

Trolling is a very effective technique whereby boat anglers can present a variety of lures over a wide-ranging area. It's particularly useful when fish are spread out and you've got to search for them. It's a leisurely type of fishing, for once the outfits have been rigged and the lures set out behind the boat, it then becomes a waiting game as you probe the waters in search of the favorite four.

Anglers seeking the striper, bluefish, weakfish, and fluke in protected bay and river waters generally fish from small boats, ranging from cartop aluminum hulls with 9.5 outboards to boats in the 20-foot range, which are ideally suited to quiet, protected waters. The general rule is that bigger is better when fishing the open reaches of ocean, sound, and bay waters, where winds can often cause heavy seas. Thus it's wise to venture forth only with a seaworthy hull, with boats in the 24-foot and larger size preferred for open water.

It's important that your boat be equipped with all of the prescribed safety gear, including electronics such as a VHF radio and radar. Important from a fishing perspective is either LORAN (long range aid to navigation) or GPS (global positioning system). Both enable you to pinpoint an exact location, which is important when you hook fish trolling, for you are then able to return to the exact same spot, often resulting in additional strikes.

A fishfinder with a color screen is another important tool of the small-boat angler trolling for stripers, blues, and weaks. The fishfinder shows schools of bait and the exact depth at which the bait is located. Frequently it will show the fish as well. Using a fishfinder in concert with LORAN or GPS, you can easily work the area where schools of fish are located, while the surrounding water is devoid of bait or fish.

The fishfinder also proves helpful in pinpointing underwater lumps, ridges, rock piles, and wrecks. Spots like this hold an abundance of bait and, in turn, the targeted species.

Downriggers, designed to take your lure to a desired depth, and permitting the strike of a fish to release the line from the downrigger, are also handy to have as part of your boat's equipment, particularly if you plan to do extensive deep-water trolling for stripers and blues.

Trolling Tackle and Techniques

Trolling for the favorite four generally results in catches ranging in weight from 3 or 4 pounds on up to the 20s, with a few fish that top 30 pounds. To maximize your enjoyment, it's best to select medium-weight trolling tackle while fishing big water. All too often anglers go forth with 50-pound gear that's so overpowering, it results in fish being hauled in with little or no enjoyment. A 6- to 7-foot-long graphite rod, rated for 20- to 30-pound line, is more than adequate. With a reel loaded with 200 to 250 yards of 30-pound-test monofilament or Dacron line, you're well prepared for even a world-record striper.

There are many areas where a combination of deep water and swift currents, with fish holding in the depths, requires the use of wire line to keep your lures within the range of the fish. This requires a 300-foot-long shot of either solid stainless-steel or Monel trolling wire, or stainless-steel cable. Each type of wire has its advantages, and ultimately it's a matter of personal choice which you prefer to use. Many anglers spool 30-pound test, although some feel 50-pound test is better because it's heavier and gets deeper quicker.

Jim Campbell landed the 35-pound striped bass held by Jack Noll, by trolling a red tube lure on wire line off Montauk, Long Island, aboard the *Sea Lion II.*

If your fishing efforts are primarily in the protected reaches of bays and rivers, then by all means select a basic popping outfit, something 6 to 6 1/2 feet long. Lean toward a graphite rod with a stiff rather than a soft action, and mount a multiplying casting reel on it loaded with 150 to 200 yards of 15-pound-test monofilament or Spectra fiber line. An outfit like this will serve you well for trolling fluke and catching big blues and stripers.

It's important to note that while trolling you're best served by a conventional multiplying reel. Spinning reels are designed for casting, and have only limited applications for the types of trolling normally employed for the favorite four.

Perhaps the most important advice to a newcomer to trolling is to mark your lines at regular intervals. Depending on the line used, you can use nail polish to mark lines, although most prefer to use sewing thread tightly wound at intervals. A good rule of thumb is to mark the line at 50-foot intervals, with a single mark at 50 feet, two marks at 100 feet, three marks at 150 feet, and four marks at 200 feet. Only by having your lines marked do you really know how far behind the boat your lures are being fished. It also proves extremely helpful once you find a school of fish and receive strikes: As you land fish you can return the lures to their same position behind the boat. Arbitrarily letting line out to what you think is the right distance is very unreliable and will handicap your ability to score.

Having wire lines marked is equally important, if not more so, for often the wire and lure are fished just inches off the bottom; too long a length of wire will snag the bottom, while too short will be far above where the fish are feeding. Using a short piece of soft telephone wire effectively marks wire lines. Use a haywire twist to wind the trolling wire and the telephone wire together at the intervals noted. It makes a neat marker and won't slide on the wire. In the event of a tangle, or if you need to cut back on the wire line, the markers can be easily removed and repositioned.

There are a variety of terminal rigs employed while trolling. The most popular consists of tying a ball-bearing swivel and coastlock snap to the terminal end of your line, whether it be wire, Spectra, or monofilament. Although not always necessary, a torpedo-shaped bead-chain trolling sinker can be attached to the coastlock snap. The sinker's weight varies, depending on the depth of water fished; for the most part they range from 1/2 through 6 ounces.

When you're probing water from 20 to 60 feet deep, a planer is often more effective than a trolling sinker. A planer is comprised of two parts. The keel is comprised of a torpedo-shaped trolling sinker, with stainless-steel delta-shaped wings extending out from the sinker. A movable arm extends from the top, as opposed to from the front as with a conventional trolling sinker. The snap swivel is attached to the arm, and the leader and lure are attached to a swivel at the rear of the planer. As it enters the water, the forward movement of the boat pulls the delta wing into the depths. At times it becomes virtually impossible to retrieve the planer and lure combo without stopping the boat. If, however, a fish strikes the lure, it trips the planer from the rear, removing the pressure and enabling you to fight the fish with ease.

Planers are available in a variety of weights and sizes, from 1 to 10 ounces. They exert tremendous pressure on the rod and reel but effectively take your lures to the desired depth. They're especially effective when schools of blues are located 30 to 40 feet deep on your fishfinder. Use of a planer accomplishes much the same objective as wire line in getting the lure deep. Many feel the planer makes for more enjoyable fishing, and is more manageable than wire line. When a fish is hooked, the planer is tripped, releasing the pressure that took it into the depths.

A fluorocarbon leader is next. Fluorocarbon is superior to monofilament because it has a much lower refractive index—approaching zero in high-quality fluorocarbon. The refractive index is a measurement of light, and fluorocarbon is virtually invisible in the water, making it more desirable as a leader material.

The author unhooks a small bluefish for granddaughter Kelsey Rosko, who hooked it while trolling a swimming plug in Barnegat Bay, New Jersey.

Use a surgeon's end loop or Bimini twist at one end, which makes for ease in slipping it onto the eye of the trolling sinker. At the terminal end of the leader use a coastlock snap or duolock snap to attach your lure. Some anglers prefer not to use a snap, and the lure may be attached to the leader using a uni-knot.

As a general rule, leaders ranging in length from 6 to 8 feet enable you to reel a fish to the transom of the boat; by taking one or two steps toward the bow and lifting the rod tip, you can then net or gaff the fish.

Some anglers go to extremes, using 15-foot leaders of 50-pound test when seeking big stripers and blues in deep ocean waters. Often this becomes impractical; it necessitates handlining the leader to get a fish within range of the gaff or net. It's often done aboard charter boats to maximize the catch, but leaves much to be desired from a sporting standpoint.

Length and pound test of the leader are determined by the type of fishing you're doing. With the type of medium tackle discussed earlier, for most situations you'd be well served using 30-pound-test fluorocarbon. If the bass and blues are running consistently large and you're using bunker spoons, umbrella rigs, and other large lures, you may want to move up to 50-pound test.

If weakfish, school stripers, and fluke are the target in protected bays and rivers, leaders of 15- to 20-pound test are fine.

Still another popular method of rigging a trolling leader is to begin by tying a three-way swivel directly to the end of your line. To one eye of the swivel tie a piece of monofilament that has a lower breaking test than your primary line. This may range from 6 inches to 3 feet in length, depending on the water depth. A dipsey-style sinker is tied to the end of the monofilament, with sizes ranging from 1/2 ounce for bays and rivers to 8 ounces in the depths of ocean and sound waters.

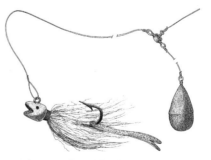

The fluorocarbon leader is attached to the remaining eye of the swivel, as discussed earlier. It can range from 3 feet in length when inshore fishing, in the 15- to 20-pound-test range, to longer, heavier leaders when targeting heavier fish in deep water.

A leadhead jig with either a bucktail or plastic tail, dressed with a strip of pork rind and sent into the depths with a 6- to 8-ounce dipsey-style sinker, is very effective when trolling in deep water.

The boat fisherman who trolls has a greater range of lures available than anglers who cast or jig. In addition, the troller has the opportunity to troll natural baits, such as strip baits for fluke and weakfish, and sandworms or eels for stripers. With all the options in lures and techniques available, and covering a lot of area, the troller often enjoys fine catches.

Don Bingler created the popular Bingle Banana, available in clear, blue, red, and green. It's an excellent trolling lure but can also be jigged effectively.

The lures that find greatest popularity among trollers are subsurface swimming plugs, spoons, leadhead jigs, metal squids, rigged eels, tube lures, and trolling feathers or their modern-day counterparts with vinyl or plastic skirts.

Another popular lure type is the umbrella rig. This rig received its name as a result of its resemblance to the wire frame of an umbrella. Some umbrella rigs have 12 small tube lures attached to the arms, with either one or two additional tubes or other lures attached to 3-foot leaders that trail behind the rig. Variations include single-arm umbrella rigs with four tubes on the arm, with a single lure trailing. There's also the daisy chain rig, comprised of four or five trolling feathers or vinyl-shell squids rigged on a single leader, separated at 12-inch intervals.

Umbrella rigs annually account for huge catches of striped bass and bluefish. Often four or more fish are hooked simultaneously, with a tangled mass of fish being brought to the boat. Many sportsmen would rather not catch fish than resort to this technique, which many deem barely a step removed from commercial fishing.

The forward motion of the boat gives the action to the majority of lures employed by trollers, such as swimming plugs, spoons, tube lures, and metal squids. An exception is the leadhead jig, which usually produces best when trolled at regular speed while you impart a jigging action to it.

Before you begin fishing, make certain to take the time to check the drag setting on your reels. Remember that a tremendous amount of pressure is exerted on the tackle as you troll along with a lot of line in the water. Too tight a drag can result in a broken line, and too light a drag may fail to set the hook. Experience will tell you what's right. Far better to have the fish take a little line than to snub it up too quickly. Once the drag is set, set the audible click on the reel, which signals a strike. Only after you've forgotten to do so will you quickly be brought to reality as you glance back and see an outfit spooled by a fish you hadn't realized you'd hooked.

On approaching the area you plan to troll, ease back on the throttle until you're at a speed of 3 to 4 knots. Place your lure in the water and hold it alongside the boat, watching its action. Plugs, metal squids, and spoons should have a swimming, side-to-side action. If they're spinning, you're going too fast. If they're moving listlessly through the water, just hanging there, you're going too slowly. Adjust your throttle accordingly.

When the lure is working to your liking, ease it back into the water, noting the distance behind the boat. For example, if you're fishing in 30 feet of water with a 6-ounce trolling sinker, swimming plug, and 150 feet of line, your lure should be in the lower half of the water column. The depth at which it's working will vary with conditions; you've got to compensate accordingly.

When you're heading into the wind and current, there are times when you'll literally be staying in one position, regardless of the speed shown on the tachometer. Here's where you've got to advance the throttle to move ahead. Conversely, when you're going with the tide and wind, ease back until the engine is barely turning over and your lures will be working just fine: You're being propelled at just the right speed by wind and current.

There will be times when all the strikes are received when you're traveling in one particular direction, especially where there's a lump off the bottom or a rip line churning.

In a rip in particular, just stemming the tide will present your lure into the churning rips and eddies; strikes will come as the fish feed. It's not unusual, however, when there's an extreme sea building as a result of the rip, to retrieve your lures, move well up into the current, turn the boat, and troll down the entire length of the rip line—in some cases a mile or longer—catching fish its entire length.

Most boatmen have the beam to fish two or three outfits in rod holders, keeping the lines well spread. When all of the lines are placed the same distance behind the boat, with the same lure and trolling sinker weight, they're all working essentially the same. Make a slow turn to port and the inside or port line will drop deeper into the water, its speed slowing, while the starboard or outboard line rises deeper in the water and speeds up. All the while the outfit in the center rod holder will maintain an average speed and the same depth.

When you receive a strike during a turn, pay attention to which line produced the strike and compensate with your speed accordingly. If, as in the above example, the port line received the strike, it was traveling deep and slow. To compensate on another pass, ease back on the throttle. This will place all three of your lures in the zone that received the first strike.

Of all the lures in the troller's arsenal, the leadhead jig is one of the most productive, especially if you take the time to work it properly by jigging the rod. This is work, and takes time and patience, but jigging the rod tip causes the jig to speed ahead, then falter and flutter until it's jigged again. This irregular action excites game fish into striking that would otherwise ignore the jig just being trolled at regular speed.

A favorite technique is for anglers to stand in the stern, facing aft, placing one hand well up from the rod's forward grip and the other at the end of the rod's butt. Using a body and arm movement, with the rod pointed downward toward the water, the rod tip is jigged forward with the one hand and pushed aft with the other, resulting in the sharp movement of the jig that brings strikes.

A technique popularized at the tunnel tubes of the Chesapeake Bay Bridge-Tunnel complex consists of using the trolling rig described earlier, with a three-way swivel and dipsey sinker. The troll with a leadhead jig and pork rind begins in the shallow water near the islands where the tunnel tube begins its descent to go beneath the shipping channels. Ease the sinker to the bottom, taking care to wear a leather thumb guard to prevent any knick in the wire cable line from injuring your thumb. The idea is to keep bouncing the sinker on the bottom, and not to drag, for if you let out too much line you're apt to snag on the rocks. As the boat trolls along, continue to ease out more line as the water gets deeper, all the while bouncing the bottom. As you approach the deepest part of the channel, you'll begin slowly retrieving line; continue as you approach the island where the tunnel exits. Often the fish are in tightly packed schools, and it's not unusual to score with two or three fish on at a time. While the majority of the stripers and weaks are schoolies, be prepared for that lunker that surprises you as it wallops the small leadhead and pork rind.

This technique works particularly well along many areas of coastline, particularly in the open ocean, where there's a broken, irregular bottom with constantly varying depths. It takes attention to develop a feel for the bottom and for keeping the dipsey sinker bouncing, but the rewards are well worth the effort.

In the protected reaches of bays and rivers there is often man-made structure that offers trolling opportunities. The abutments of bridges, docks, piers, and breakwaters often hold an abundance of bait and, in turn, your quarry. Trolling in close proximity to this structure often coaxes strikes from fish that stem the tide in the rips and eddies formed by the current.

Where to Fish

Now with your boat equipped with electronics, basic outfits, and lures, and your tackle and techniques in place, you're set to move out in your quest of the favorite four—almost. There's still one important thing to do before moving out on the water: Obtain a set of coast and geodetic charts of the area you plan to fish and carefully study them.

The charts, some of which are available on computer disks, show the bottom conformation in detail. Water depths, channel edges, lumps and ridges, rock piles, points of land where rips form, and location of underwater obstructions, man-made reefs, and wrecks are clearly identified.

Trollers eager to go fishing often get in deep trouble when they're not knowledgeable about the water they plan to fish. A classic example is the Shrewsbury Rocks, located off the north Jersey coast and a haunt of striped bass and bluefish. The rocks extend up from the bottom at irregular intervals and are festooned with the lures of thousands of boatmen who didn't have their lines marked or realize where the rocks were, resulting in immediate loss of lures as they trolled into the area. Indeed, skin divers regularly dive here to retrieve the terminal tackle that succumbs to the rocks and debris that litter the area. Much the same can be said of the rock areas off Montauk Point, Long Island, the Chesapeake Bay Bridge-Tunnel complex, and myriad other spots along the coast. You've got to know and understand the water in order to be a successful troller.

There are times when all four species discussed in this book are caught over a flat, open bottom. Those occasions when an abundance of forage takes up residence in an open area are ideal for the troller, for it often becomes a matter of simply letting the lures out a specific distance behind the boat, setting the boat's speed to 3 or 4 knots, and trolling through the area until a strike is received.

More often, however, baitfish will take up residence in areas with certain peculiarities to their liking. These include the irregular bottom conformation formed at points of land, where the flow of the tidal current often builds up sandbars, with a severe drop-off into deeper water. Stripers, blues, and weaks take up stations at such spots. As the swift-flowing current clashes with the sandbars, rips of churning water form, and the bait is swept through the maelstrom to the waiting fish.

Forage species will invariably be found on almost any lump or ridge extending up from the bottom. Often you can scan your fishfinder as you travel over miles of open bottom, and not read any bait or fish. Suddenly, as a lump or ridge rises from the otherwise flat bottom, you'll have readings of schools of sand eels and other bait, along with stripers and bluefish.

The same can be said for wrecks. Sometimes the bait and fish take up station directly above a wreck, sometimes off to the side. Frequently, it looks as though both are living together peacefully—which is often the case until the heavyweights get hungry, then suddenly the bait begins to move about, as do the stripers and blues, and the carnage begins.

Rocky bottom along the coast varies from spot to spot. Sometimes a rocky bottom is relatively flat, and the attraction is the myriad cunner, sea bass, tautog, crabs, and lobsters that take up residence. While many anglers think that the favorite four eat only menhaden, mullet, herring, and mackerel, they actually eat great quantities of any small forage or even the fry of game fish.

At other times the rocks may extend up 20 to 30 feet, with jagged peaks, deep valleys, and opportunities galore for bait to congregate. When huge schools of forage aren't available, this is where you're going to find everything from stripers to fluke searching for a meal.

In bay and river waters, channel edges are still another spot where fish tend to congregate. Here currents clash with the adjoining flats, churning food on the bottom, exposing clams, crabs, shrimp, and baitfish moving with the tide. It's important to study the tide here as well, for spots that produce on a flooding tide may simply skirt a sand flat at low tide.

Always keep in mind that for every fish you see on your fishfinder near the surface, there are usually many more in the depths. Most stripers, blues, and weaks tend to stay deep, and the successful troller gets his lures deep to score. The ideal situation comes when you can use a downrigger, planer, or trolling sinker to get your lures deep. When this isn't possible, the choice moves to wire line, either Monel, solid stainless steel, or stainless-steel cable. Although wire is the least desirable line to use with respect to maximizing the sporting qual-

The bunker spoon is very effective when fished deep using wire line, particularly when striped bass and bluefish are feeding on menhaden, herring, and mackerel. The keel position is easily adjusted until a pulsating action is achieved. The spoon should not spin when trolled.

ities of the fish, it's extremely effective. In recent years many anglers have begun using stainless-steel cable as their wire of choice, because it's more easily managed than solid stainless. Its one drawback is that occasionally a strand of cable will break, leaving a burr, which can injure your thumb if you don't wear a thumb guard.

Some of the most exciting trolling for stripers, blues, and weaks occurs when the fish are on the surface chasing schools of menhaden, herring, rainfish, and mullet. Fish feeding on top, where there's often a cover of screaming, diving seagulls, are easily spooked, far more so than when they're feeding in the depths.

Exercise care when approaching a school of surface-feeding fish. You'll get more strikes by working along the perimeter of the school. Before you reach the school, make certain to adjust your terminal tackle accordingly. Remove planers or heavy trolling sinkers. If you're trolling three lines, work a couple with just 2 or 3 ounces of trolling weight and fish one line with no weight at all, so your plug, spoon, or leadhead stays near the surface. Then make adjustments as you begin to receive strikes.

While admittedly deep-water trolling is productive, some of the most exciting striper and bluefish action can be experienced while trolling the hundreds of miles of surf along the coast. Both species often feed right among the breakers, from the beach to several hundred feet offshore, and especially along the outer bars.

They'll readily strike a trolled lure, and the beauty of this fishing is that it's in water that ranges from 6 to 15 feet deep. Most often you can use monofilament or Dacron line, with just a small trolling sinker. Trolling swimming plugs, rigged eels, and bunker spoons is often very productive along the surf line. Stripers tend to move into this water toward dusk and stay right through until an hour or so after daybreak, providing exciting night trolling opportunities.

You've got to be careful, however, because incoming waves and a ground swell can be dangerous if you're not in control.

Trolling for Fluke

The trolling techniques just discussed primarily target stripers, blues, and weaks, which feed throughout the entire water column, from the bottom to the surface. Occasionally a fluke is hooked on a line being fished near the bottom with a leadhead jig or deep-running plug.

Most fluke are caught while drifting. You need wind or current for a good drift. If there's a dead calm, the troller who employs a bottom rig really scores, while the boats that aren't moving and covering lots of bottom go fishless.

You can use the same fluke rig for trolling that you use while drifting. As a rule you'll need a heavier sinker, because the forward movement while trolling will often cause a lightweight sinker to balloon off the bottom.

Tie a three-way swivel to the end of your line. Then tie in a 6-inch-long piece of monofilament line with a loop in the end of it, onto which you'll slip a dipsey- or bank-style sinker. To the remaining eye of the swivel tie a 36-inch-long piece of 20- or 30-pound-test fluorocarbon leader material. A Wide Gap–, Beak-, or Claw-style hook, in sizes ranging from 1 through 4/0, works nicely with this rig while trolling.

A live killie is a fine bait to use while trolling. Hook it through the lips and it will swim nicely on the troll. A strip of sea robin, dogfish, fluke belly, squid, or other cut bait also works well with this rig. Strip baits are usually tough and durable, and when a fluke strikes it's less apt to rip the bait from the hook. While some anglers thread a spearing or sand eel on their hook while trolling, these baits sometimes spin and twist and are not as effective as a live killie or mullet, or a strip bait that flutters.

Trolling Sandworms and Eels

Using essentially the same rig is also very effective for stripers and weakfish while using live sandworms as bait. Use a Beak- or Claw-style hook with a baitholder shank to securely hold the worm.

Thread a single large sandworm onto the hook by waiting until it opens its mouth then slipping the hook point in, threading it down 1/2 inch, and bringing it out the side. As you hold the leader, the hook and worm will hang straight.

Trolling through known striper haunts, using a light dipsey sinker, just heavy enough to bounce the bottom, and one or two sandworms as bait, regularly accounts for many stripers each season.

Another variation is to use a trolling sinker and leader, with a June Bug, Colorado, or Willowleaf spinner on the leader ahead of the sandworm bait. The fluttering spinner blade acts as an attractor, and a hungry striper or weakfish is on it in a flash.

The three-way swivel rig can also be used with a live eel. Use a size 4/0 through 6/0 Claw- or Beak-style hook and place the hook in the eel's lips. When lowered to the bottom and slowly trolled, the eel will swim enticingly as you troll along, bringing strikes from stripers, weaks, and the occasional doormat fluke. Avoid using the eel when bluefish are plentiful in an area, for you'll experience an attrition of all your eels in short order: Blues are notorious for biting the eels in half, usually missing the hook.

Trolling permits you to cover a lot of area. To score consistently using this technique requires lots of study, for it's a combination of the bottom you're fishing, concentrations of bait, stage of the tide, presentation of the lure, boat speed, and other variables that determines whether or not you'll be successful. Once you've mastered the technique, you can score regularly. Experience will teach you just where you should be at a given time and which lures and techniques will bring you strikes.

Using the proper knot is very important, especially when using light tackle to tangle with big bluefish, like this beauty landed within sight of the Statue of Liberty.

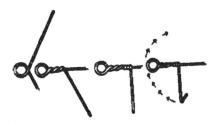

HAYWIRE TWIST

The haywire twist is used with stainless-steel leader wire to make an end loop. Begin by making a loop in the wire and holding it firmly between your thumb and index finger. Next take the thumb and index finger of your other hand and evenly twist the wire around itself at least three times. Make three or four turns with the short end of the wire neatly around the standing part of the wire. Finish by forming a small handle and using it to bend back and forth and break the wire off clean.

ALBRIGHT KNOT

The Albright knot is used for joining monofilament or fluorocarbon lines of unequal diameters, for creating shock leaders, and when a Bimini twist is tied in the end of the casting line. It's also used for connecting monofilament line to stainless-steel leader wire or the new titanium leader wire.

1. Bend a loop in the tag end of the heavier monofilament or wire and hold it between the thumb and forefinger of your left hand. Insert the tag end of the lighter monofilament through the loop from the top.

2. Slip the tag end of the lighter monofilament under your left thumb and pinch it tightly against the heavier strands of the loop. Wrap the first turn of the lighter monofilament over itself and continue wrapping toward the round end of the loop. Take at least 12 turns with the lighter monofilament around all three strands.

3. Insert the tag end of the lighter monofilament through the end of the loop from the bottom. It must enter and leave the loop on the same side.

4. With the thumb and forefinger of your left hand, slide the coils of the lighter monofilament toward the end of the loop, stopping 1/8 inch from the end of the loop. Using pliers, pull the tag end of the lighter monofilament tight to keep the coils from slipping off the loop.

5. With your left hand still holding the heavier monofilament or wire, pull on the standing part of the lighter monofilament. Pull the tag end of the lighter monofilament and the standing part a second time. Pull the standing part of the heavy monofilament or wire and the standing part of the light monofilament.

6. Trim both tag ends.

SURGEON'S KNOT

This easy-to-tie knot is popular for joining a heavy monofilament leader to a lighter monofilament main line.

1. Lay 6 to 8 inches of line and leader parallel and overlapping.

2. Using the two lines, tie an overhand knot.

3. Proceed to tie a second overhand knot.

4. Pull both lines in opposing directions to gather and tighten the knot. Trim the tag ends.

DROPPER LOOP

This is a good knot for creating one or more loops in a leader or main line for attaching hooks, jigs, or a sinker. If you want a swivel or hook inside the dropper loop, make certain to slip it in place in step 1.

1. Form a loop of the size you desire.

2. Twist the loop around the main line eight times.

3. Reach through the center of the twists and pull the loop through.

4. Hold the loop with your teeth (be careful not to nick the line), or place a pencil in the loop so it doesn't pull up too tight, while you pull on both ends of the main line to tighten the dropper loop snug.

SURGEON'S END LOOP

This is one of the simplest and quickest ways to create double lines
for splicing to heavy leader material or for tying directly to terminal tackle.

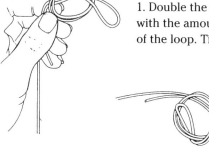

1. Double the end of the main line to form a loop,
with the amount you double determining the size
of the loop. Tie an overhand knot.

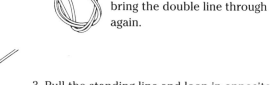

2. With the loop still open,
bring the double line through
again.

3. Pull the standing line and loop in opposite
directions to gather and tighten the knot.
Trim the tag end.

4. Once this knot is tied, create a dropper
by snipping the loop.

5. For drift fishing, use the shorter of the two
strands for a sinker, the other for a hook.

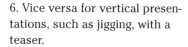

6. Vice versa for vertical presen-
tations, such as jigging, with a
teaser.

BIMINI TWIST

The strongest loop knot of all—but also the most difficult to tie—the Bimini twist is used to create double line for pursuing big saltwater fish, and is most popular with trolling rigs for big stripers and blues.

1. Measure a loop slightly more than twice the footage you want for the double line. Holding the standing line and tag end together, twist the loop about 20 times.

2. Sit down and put your legs into the loop and apply outward pressure. At the same time, pull out on the standing line and tag ends to force the twists tightly together.

3. Maintaining leg pressure, hold the standing line in one hand with the tension slightly off vertical. With the other hand, move the tag end to a right angle from the twists and gradually ease tension. The tag end should begin to roll over the twists.

4. Continue outward leg pressure on the loop. Steer the tag end into a tight downward spiral over the twists.

5. Continue to maintain leg pressure once the tag end reaches the bottom of the twists. With the hand that has been holding the standing end, place your index finger in the crotch of the line where the loop joins the knot to prevent any slippage of the last turn. Make a half hitch with the tag end around one strand of the loop and pull it tight.

6. With the half hitch holding the knot you can release leg pressure, but keep the loop stretched out. With the remaining tag end, make a half hitch around both strands of the loop, but do not pull tight.

7. Take two more turns around both strands of the loop, winding inside the bend of the line formed by the loose half hitch and toward the main knot. Put the tag end through the bend of the loose half hitch created in step 6.

8. Pull the tag end to gather and tighten the loops around the main knot. Trim the tag end.

IMPROVED CLINCH KNOT

This is one of the most common of all fishing knots, perhaps because of the simplicity of tying it. For still greater strength you can double the end of your line with a surgeon's loop and then tie the improved clinch knot with the doubled line.

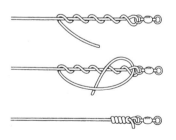

1. Pull the line through the eye of a swivel and double back, making five turns around the standing line.

2. Holding the coils, pull the tag end through the loop closest to the eye, and then back through the big loop you just created.

3. Slide the knot tight and trim the tag end.

SNELLING A HOOK

This method of snelling a hook is really a variation of the uni-knot and makes a neat, strong connection between leader and hook.

1. Thread the line or leader about 6 inches through the hook eye. Hold the line against the hook shank and form a uni-knot circle.

2. Make five or six turns through the loop and around the leader and hook shank as desired. Close the knot by pulling on the tag end of the line.

3. Tighten by pulling the standing line in one direction and the hook in the other.

BLOOD KNOT

This is one of the best knots for joining two monofilament lines of similar diameters—or for joining two dissimilar-diameter lines by doubling the lighter of the two.

1. Overlap the two parallel lines by 12 inches total. Take five wraps on one side and pull the end back through between the two strands.

2. Repeat on the other side, pulling the other end through the strands in the opposite direction.

3. Pull the two tag ends slowly to gather the knot.

4. Once gathered neatly, pull the standing line to tighten the knot. Trim the tag ends.

UNI-KNOT

This is a strong, versatile knot that can also be tied to form an end loop that tightens down to a conventional knot once you hook a fish.

1. Run 6 inches of line
through the eye
and fold it back
to make two parallel lines.

2. Bring the tag end back
toward the eye and make
six spiral wraps around the
two parallel lines.

3. Snug the knot; to leave a loop, hold
the knot at the point where you want it
while you pull on the standing line.

4. If you don't want a loop, slide the knot to the eye.
Trim the tag end.

THE UNI-KNOT SYSTEM

This knot can be used in a variety of applications, including the joining of two lines, as shown here.

1. Overlap the ends of two lines of about the same diameter for about 6 inches. With one end, form a uni-knot circle, crossing the two lines about midway of their overlapped distance.

2. Tie a uni-knot, making six turns around the two lines.

3. Pull the tag end to snug the knot tight around the line.

4. Use the loose end of overlapped line to tie another uni-knot and snug up.

5. Pull the two standing lines in opposite directions to slide the knots together. Pull as tight as possible and snip the ends close to the nearest coil.

6

During the course of a season the boatman seeking inshore gamefish will be presented with a variety of situations. There are times when in crowded waterways you'll get readings of large concentrations of fish right on the bottom. On other occasions you'll see a display of surface action as stripers, blues, and weaks attack baitfish from below. Often the frightened forage leap skyward to avoid the attack from below, only to be targeted from above by screaming, diving gulls. Both situations offer bonanza fishing, vertically jigging for the deep dwellers and casting to the surface-feeding fish.

Tackle and techniques

Given the choice, most anglers prefer a multiplying reel for vertical jigging and a spinning reel for casting. The multiplying reel gives you better control, although some spinning devotees challenge that opinion. It's important that you be comfortable with the tackle you elect to use.

For most inshore bay and river situations, a good rule of thumb is to use a graphite popping-style rod in the 6- to 7-foot-long size, with a somewhat stiff action rather than soft. It should be capable of handling lures in the 1/2- through 2-ounce range. A quality multiplying reel with a star drag capable of holding 150 to 200 yards of 12- to 15-pound-test monofilament is ideal. An outfit such as this is capable of landing any of the favorite four, providing your equipment is in good order and you take your time with a big fish.

For deep-water jigging, especially in ocean and sound waters, it's best to move up to a heavier outfit. You've often got to use 6- or 8-ounce jigs to reach the fish in 40 to 60 feet of water, where wind and current push you along at fast speed. A graphite rod measuring 7 feet in length with a stiff action, rather than soft, is a good choice. Move up to a reel that will hold 150 to 200 yards of 20- or 30-pound-test monofilament and you're set.

It's advantageous to use a leader when vertical jigging, rather than tying the lure directly to your line. For the popping outfit use 20- or 30-pound-test fluorocarbon. A 40-pound-test leader is appropriate for the heavier outfit. While you may get by without a leader, the terminal end—either with a leader or just the line—takes a lot of abuse while fighting a fish, from the teeth of blues, weaks, and fluke to the sharp gill covers and scales of stripers, hence the advantage of a leader.

A small black barrel swivel may be used to join the line and leader with a uni-knot. This is the preferred method if you plan to use a teaser in conjunction with the primary lure. Some anglers prefer to double the terminal end of their line with a surgeon's loop and then use a surgeon's knot to tie the leader to the double line, eliminating the need for a swivel.

To the terminal end of the leader tie a small duolock snap; this facilitates lure changing.

If you plan to use a teaser for vertical jigging, which is strongly recommended, tie your leader following the instructions provided in chapter 11.

Many anglers prefer using a wire leader if bluefish dominate the area being fished. No. 8 or 9 stainless-steel wire is a popular choice; use with care when employing a haywire twist to form connections. The wire will save you lures that would otherwise be lost to sharp teeth severing the monofilament or fluorocarbon leader.

A chrome-plated or stainless-steel diamond jig is, along with Vike or Hopkins jigs, without question the most popular for vertical jigging. The diamond jig is available in models ranging from 1/2 ounce to 16 ounces. For purposes of catching the favorite four, the top-end weight you're apt to need is 8 ounces. There are also many jigs molded of lead in the shape of a fish, then airbrushed in detail to replicate a small baitfish, and they're very effective.

The Hopkins Shorty is made of hammered stainless steel and will bring strikes from the favorite four while casting from boat or beach. It's also effective as a trolled lure or when probing the depths while jigging.

Many of these jigs are marketed with treble hooks. A case can be made for the hooking effectiveness of trebles. They do make hook removal very difficult, and in fact make it virtually impossible to unhook fish without harming them. In view of minimum size restrictions in place for many of the species covered in this book, it's advantageous to forgo use of trebles on jigs.

A good choice is to replace the treble with an O'Shaughnessy-style single hook, preferably with a plastic tube tail in red, green, or purple.

Leadhead jigs with a soft plastic tail are another popular lure for vertical jigging, as is the bucktail jig. Sizes range from 1/4 ounce to 4 ounces for the applications discussed here. A wide variety of plastic tails is available to the angler, many shaped and colored to resemble sand eels, spearing, mullet, mackerel, and other small forage. The plastic tails draw many strikes, but bluefish have a reputation for biting them off just behind the hook. A bucktail jig is better when you're seeking the choppers, because it's more durable.

This big weakfish struck a leadhead jig and strip of pork rind in the waters off Virginia Beach, Virginia, where the Chesapeake Bay meets the Atlantic.

When using a bucktail jig, many anglers enhance its action with a strip of pork rind. Tail-hook pork rind—which, as its name implies, has a hook in the middle of the tail section—is especially effective when fish strike short, missing the primary hook of the lure. The tail hook almost always gets the short striker.

Plugs don't lend themselves to vertical jigging, with the exception of mirror plugs and rattle-type plugs. Neither of these plugs has a lip; the eye that's attached to the leader is on the top of the plug's head. As such, they may be worked much like a jig. Most are in 1/4- through 2-ounce sizes and are very effective in inshore waters, but aren't heavy enough for jigging in deep ocean waters.

Plugs of this type are customarily equipped with a treble hook in the belly and one in the tail. Most anglers seeking the species being discussed use a pair of pliers and bend down the barbs, which makes removal of the hook and subsequent release of small fish relatively easy.

Using a teaser in conjunction with any of the aforementioned jigs and plugs puts you at a decided advantage. A Clouser saltwater fly tied on a 3/0 hook with an epoxy head is an ideal choice. The weight of its head holds it away from the leader and gives it an independent action as it's jigged. Colors such as brown and white with a trace of gold Mylar, chartreuse and white with silver Mylar, and blue and white with silver Mylar all produce well, depending on the bait in the area.

Another fine saltwater fly to use as a teaser is the Lefty's Deceiver. Popularized by noted angler Lefty Kreh, it has accounted for many fine catches. When the fish are schooled up and chasing bait they're often in such a voracious feeding frenzy that they'll strike a teaser made of a tuft of bucktail tied to a 3/0 or 4/0 O'Shaughnessy hook.

There are literally hundreds of saltwater flies tied to resemble forage species, and most of them work nicely when used as a teaser.

You can also use a plastic bait tail as a teaser, slipping it on a 3/0 or 4/0 hook. Many soft plastic baits are molded and colored to exactly duplicate a live baitfish. The sand eel model is such a close replica that when placed side by side with a real sand eel it's difficult to tell the difference.

The single most important consideration in working any of the diamond jigs, plugs, and leadheads is to make the lure appear to be a struggling, helpless, wounded baitfish. All predatory species are apt to feed on prey easy to engulf, rather than healthy fry swimming normally. As such it's necessary to "jig" or work the lure whenever it's in the water.

All too often newcomers to jigging simply let their lure settle into the depths then reel it back up, with a lackluster appearance. It's far better to ease the jig into the water, permit it to settle 5 or 6 feet, then apply thumb pressure on the line spool and lift back smartly with your rod tip. This results in the jig settling, then darting to the surface, faltering, and settling again. Repeat this procedure until the jig reaches the bottom, unless you receive a strike on the way down. Invariably this technique results in far more strikes than the jig free-falling to the bottom.

Once you feel the jig touch bottom, lock your reel into gear, lift the rod tip smartly again, and begin reeling. Retrieve 5 or 6 feet of line, then smartly lift the rod tip; continue retrieving and jigging until you reach the surface.

As you go through these steps, vary the speed of your drop and retrieve. Often bluefish will strike a fast-moving lure, while stripers and weaks appear to prefer a slower-moving jig. You'll find times when the aforementioned procedure should be set aside in favor of speed-reeling the jig, working it as fast as you can, which is especially productive when the blues are in a feeding frenzy.

While varying the procedure and speed you'll suddenly find that you're receiving strikes with a given pattern, and often at a given depth. Then it's important to adjust, and often forgo working the lure to the strike zone. Instead, just let it drop, and work within the range where the fish are feeding.

Many of the new saltwater jigging reels have depth counters on them. By watching the counter you'll know precisely the depth at which a fish is hooked; on succeeding drops you can adjust accordingly. This is very helpful, and saves wasted effort, particularly when you're fishing on an offshore hill or lump where the water is 50 or 60 feet deep, but the fish are feeding at the 40-foot level in the water column.

Keeping the line perpendicular to the bottom generally produces the best results, with the jig working vertically. There are times when a fast drift makes this difficult. Then it's best to fish from the down-current side of the boat, casting your jig out and away from the boat, in the direction of the drift. As it settles, you'll be drifting toward it; most of your drop and retrieve will be nearly perpendicular.

This is not to say that vertical jigging is the only way to go. There are times when all three species may be feeding very near or right on the surface. On these occasions it's certainly appropriate to cast any of the jigs, plugs, or leadheads and use a steady retrieve while varying your speed until you find the combination that produces.

If the fish are feeding from the surface to a depth of 10 feet a whip retrieve often works well, too. Cast out, permit the lure to settle, and then use a combination of reeling and working your rod tip to cause the jig to dart ahead and falter.

A variation on the leadhead and bucktail jigs is the ball jig. As its name implies, the ball jig—and its cousin the bullet jig—are molded of lead in either a ball or bullet shape. They have an eye to which your leader is tied, and a free-swinging single hook dressed with bucktail or a plastic skirt. Ball and bullet jigs come in a variety of sizes, ranging from 1/4 ounce to 2 ounces. You'll get the best results by using a weight sufficiently heavy to keep it perpendicular to the bottom as you drift along, lifting the rod tip, and causing the jig to bounce the bottom. Adding a strip of squid to the hook enhances its action.

Jigging for Fluke

Fluke at times will feed throughout the entire water column. They'll actually chase bait right on the surface. For the most part, however, they prefer to probe along the bottom, or a couple of feet above it, to satisfy their appetites.

Among the most popular lures for jigging fluke are those that can be effectively worked right along the bottom, either while anchored or drifting. The leadhead jig with a plastic tail and the bucktail jig are unquestionably the two most popular jigs for anglers seeking flatfish. Leadheads ranging from 1/4 ounce to 3 ounces can be brought into play, depending on the depth of water and speed of the drift. A proper-sized leadhead will plummet to the bottom, and can be effectively worked in one of two ways. The most popular method is to gently lift your rod tip, causing the jig to rise off the bottom and then settle back down. Alternating the speed of the jigging motion helps until you find the combination that brings strikes.

Using a dead-stick approach also accounts for many summer flounder each season. A small leadhead with a plastic tail is lowered to the bottom and the rod is placed in a rod holder, with the drift and bouncing movement of the boat providing the action. While it's not as much fun as holding the rod and working the jig, you'll often be pleasantly surprised at the number of strikes a dead stick receives.

Many fluke fishermen use a ball or bullet jig instead of a sinker. It becomes the bottom hook on their rig; they then tie off a second hook via a dropper loop 15 to 20 inches above the jig. In this way you get the best of both worlds, employing a jig on the bottom while still having a natural bait such as a live killie, spearing, or strip bait drifting above it.

The rattle plug is another flounder lure that's particularly effective for jigging the shallow reaches of bays and rivers. Let it settle to the bottom and then just keep working your rod tip, causing the plug to slip and slide along the bottom, emitting its rattling noise, which attracts flatfish.

Casting Tackle and Techniques

Although jigging has its devotees and is surely a very effective technique, there are often times when casting a lure presents exciting opportunities when jigging just wouldn't work.

Myriad possibilities exist, ranging from random casting on the open bay and ocean to probing shallow shorelines and casting to rock outcroppings, bridge towers, the shadow line of bridges at night, and the rips and eddies formed at points of land and around man-made docks, breakwaters, and the like.

Casting to the shoreline from a drifting boat also offers many possibilities. There are thousands of miles of bay, river, and ocean shoreline along the Atlantic coast, and almost every inch holds a population of forage, including small fish, crabs, shrimp, squid, sand bugs, and other food. The forage hugs the shallows, where waves crash on the beach or marsh grass offers protection. A lure cast to the shoreline and retrieved toward deeper water is certain to draw strikes. Often you can work miles of shoreline, picking all four species as you do, using a wide range of the smaller casting lures.

Striped bass and weakfish are notorious for stemming the tide—facing into the current and holding their positions—with their nose tight to the shadow line of bridge and dock lights at night. In many areas you can stem the tide with your boat, holding your position with your bow into the current and just enough speed to stay in place. Sometimes you'll see dozens of fish, all facing into the tidal flow, waiting for shrimp, crabs, and forage fish to be swept their way. Just watching them is fun, for they'll dart out and engulf a morsel being swept along, then quickly return to their position, waiting for another treat to be swept their way.

The key is stemming the tide with your boat, often beneath the span, and casting your lure up into the current. Quartering the current is also often effective: Cast your lure at a 45-degree angle up into the current, and retrieve it toward the shadow line, where the fish, sometimes two or three of them, will dart out to engulf it.

The lights of the bridges and docks so illuminate the water that you'll see bluefish chasing bait on the surface while the air is alive with screaming, diving seagulls. Small popping plugs, swimmers, leadhead jigs, and Hopkins bring immediate strikes.

Another exciting casting possibility is fishing a point of land. This can range from the tip of a huge peninsula to a 100-foot-long point extending out into the bay. In both situations there will be a flow of current parallel with the beach until it reaches the point, where the current and flow of water will be restricted, causing a rip or eddy. Sometimes there's a 6-foot-high wall of water as the tide flows seaward, causing a pronounced rip line with heavy white water on one side and placid water on the other. The stripers, blues, and weaks will often take up stations in the quiet water, where they expend little energy, simply waiting for the current to carry their meal to them, darting into the maelstrom to pick a morsel as it drifts within range.

It's often possible to either drift with the current—taking care not to put the boat and you in harm's way by being too near the heavy water—or stem the tide, with each providing the opportunity to work a variety of lures through the rip and along its edges.

Popping plugs, surface and subsurface swimming plugs, darters, leadhead jigs, and metal squids all come into their own when you're casting. Balance your tackle and lure sizes to the situation. For casting in the protected reaches of bays and rivers, a one-handed spinning outfit or a popping outfit is ideal. In the open ocean, where conditions dictate heavier gear, move up to moderate tackle, rated for 15- to 20-pound-test line, for maximum sport. All too often anglers tend to go much too heavy when casting or jigging for the favorite four, which takes away from the enjoyment.

Where to Fish

As a general rule, you'll have more opportunities to target fish feeding in the depths than on the surface. The situation may develop in a coastal river, broad expanse of bay, or the vast inshore ocean. When you mark large fish in the depths, the electronic fishfinder will often show schools of forage as well. The sand eels, rainfish, menhaden, and mackerel will often show as a cloud, often hovering at mid-depths.

Where ranges make it difficult to pinpoint an exact location, using your LORAN or GPS to mark the position is important. It's frustrating to go over fish, feeling you can double back, only to lose your bearings because you forgot to mark the fish. Although the fish may move, if you mark their location when you first spot them, you can cruise in an ever-widening circle from where the fish were until you find them again.

You're apt to find schooling fish in the same areas where the bait tends to congregate. While on occasion the fish will be herding bait over a flat, open bottom, more often than not there's some sort of structure. Rocky outcroppings extending up from the bottom are a

The entrance to a tunnel of the Chesapeake Bay Bridge-Tunnel complex forms the backdrop as anglers cast to the rips formed on an outgoing tide.

typical example. Ridges, or what might be termed underwater hills, are another gathering place for baitfish, and in turn your quarry. At points of land there are often rips, eddies, and abrupt drop-offs in water depths where fish take up residence in the quiet water, waiting for food to be swept their way.

By carefully reviewing geodetic charts you can ascertain these spots in the general area you plan to fish. While the spots are important, it's also significant to remember that the stage of the tide and the current it forms play a role in the movements of the fish. You can probe a location for hours and your fishfinder screen will be blank; then suddenly both bait and feeding fish will light up the screen with readings. Changing conditions, most often the current, are what cause the movements.

Many anglers carry a 1-gallon milk jug to which is tied a length of 130-pound-test Dacron and a 16-ounce sinker. This makes a very effective marker buoy and can be dropped immediately once fish are located.

The key to determining where to begin a drift is observing the wind and current and positioning your boat to carry you to the fish. Depending on its strength, wind may be the determining factor, while on a windless day the current will carry you.

Frequently anglers err in positioning their boat directly over the fish; before they can present their lures the boat will have drifted off from where the fish are feeding. It's usually best to shut down 100 feet or more from where the fish are and drift into them. You're also less apt to spook them with a drift approach.

As you drift through the fish, and hopefully score, you'll just as quickly drift away from them. Be alert: As soon as the fishfinder goes blank, reposition yourself, making a circular approach so as to not run over and spook the feeding fish.

Casting to rocky outcroppings—along the Maine coast, the submerged rocks of Montauk, the myriad jetties that extend seaward along the Jersey coast, the riprap of the Chesapeake Bay Bridge-Tunnel complex—offers exciting opportunities. Baitfish tend to congregate around any rocks, wrecks, pilings, or other obstructions that offer sanctuary from open water.

Stripers, blues, and weaks know this, and they cruise along such spots, waiting and watching for any unsuspecting baitfish that leaves its lair. Anglers fishing from small boats can move within casting range, place their lures tight to the rocks, and retrieve them, which gives the appearance of a small baitfish moving into open water.

Almost all of the lures discussed throughout this book may be used in this kind of situation, including plugs, leadheads, metal squids, and the myriad small metal lures molded to resemble those baitfish found in the area being fished.

Jigging or casting is work: Make no mistake about it. While the bottom fisherman and troller enjoy the leisurely sport of fishing-and-relaxing, the jigging or casting devotee is probing all the time. It's an exciting challenge, and very satisfying, for when you score you know it's a direct result of having presented a lure that fooled the favorite four into striking.

7

DRIFTING

It's difficult to put into words the peace and solitude you experience while drifting the waters of a shallow coastal bay. There are the seagulls, circling and diving to pick an unsuspecting spearing from the surface. A mallard swims by with her brood of 12 swimmming feverishly to keep up. The afternoon breeze is refreshing and cooling—a respite from the sun high in the summer sky. The wind and tidal flow move you along as you enjoy the great outdoors.

Scenes like this are repeated daily through the season from the Carolinas on north to Maine. Sometimes it's on a quiet, meandering coastal river, or on the broad expanse of a threatening ocean, where whitecaps fleck the surface. Settings like these set the stage for the contemplative side of fishing, being outdoors and enjoying nature's bounty.

Tackle and Techniques

Many are the stories that could be told of two boats setting forth for a day of drift fishing for the favorite four. One returns with a fine catch while the other's fish box is clean. Most often the reason is because one set off with a plan while the other arbitrarily drifted along, hoping to score.

Drift fishing takes patience, study of the water you plan to fish, understanding tidal flow and the role it plays in the movement of fish, applying your knowledge of bait movements, and skills in presenting a bait or lure to the favorite four.

Understanding tidal flow is especially important with drift fishing. It determines just which way you'll be drifting, except in those instances when wind conditions overpower the movement of the current. Almost every tackle shop along the seacoast has tide charts available, which show the exact stage of tide at a given spot, right down to the minute. Within just a matter of a few miles, ranging from the open ocean to the protected reaches of a large bay, there may be a difference of four or five hours between the times of high tide.

Something many fail to understand is that the tide charts generally show the times of high tide and low tide only. The times noted represent the vertical movement of water, or the upper or lower extremes of the depth of water at a given time. This serves a purpose for boatmen, who may want to traverse an area when the water reaches its highest level. Often this confuses fishermen, however, in that they assume that at high tide there's also slack water. This isn't the case. It just means that the water has reached the highest level it will achieve.

At the time of high tide, when the water level reaches its highest vertical movement, the current continues to flow laterally, moving water into back rivers and bays, but the height of the water remains the same. Just when slack tide occurs varies widely. Sometimes the difference in time between high tide and slack tide is just a few minutes. The East River off Manhattan, New York, is a case in point, where in a matter of minutes the direction in which the water is flowing changes.

At other spots, such as the Bay Head Canal that joins the Manasquan River in New Jersey with Barnegat Bay, the lateral tidal flow will continue for more than an hour before slack water is finally achieved; all the while, as the current is moving, the water height does not change.

It's the slack-water periods that play a major role in fishing, because during the middle of the tide, when the water is flowing at its swiftest, fish often tend to become less active, taking up stations in rips and eddies or moving to the quiet-water areas less affected by current. This applies to movements of both bait and the game fish being sought. As the water movement slows, the activity begins, with the favorite four frequently moving great distances to feed leisurely without having to combat the swift current they would have experienced earlier.

Slack-water tables are available for most of the major harbors along the coast, because they play an important role where tugs must maneuver big ships into docks. They're generally not available for the small coves, rivers, and bays where you may do your fishing. As a result, many veteran anglers prepare their own slack-water tables for the areas they regularly fish. These are used in concert with the regular tide charts that indicate high tide and low tide. Through experience and following their tables, they know precisely when the tide will be slack at favorite spots and plan their drifting, bottom fishing, casting, and trolling strategies accordingly.

The striped bass, bluefish, weakfish, and fluke often take up residence in the same waters. Indeed, it's not unusual to catch all four species on a given day, from a very small area. Catching all four species in a day has come to be known as a Northeast Super Grand Slam, a sterling accomplishment when you set out specifically to do it.

Drift fishing is perhaps the best technique to employ should you set your sights on a Northeast Super Grand Slam—to catch one each of the favorite four on a given day—or even a Northeast Grand Slam, three of the four species. It's a personal challenge to do this, and it's not easily done.

It's best accomplished by recognizing that the four targeted species are often traveling and feeding in different parts of the water column. The fluke may be resting on the bottom, waiting for a meal; blues may be giving menhaden fits as they're driven to leaping from the water to escape the vicious teeth. Stripers and weakfish are often somewhere in between.

Not surprisingly, many boatmen set out for a day of "bluefishing" or "fluking" and basically end up catching the targeted species. Little do they realize that they're drifting over known haunts of other species, which can easily be caught while still seeking the targeted blues or fluke.

DRIFTING THE DEAD STICK

There's a practice commonly called dead-sticking by small-boat anglers. In essence, assume four or five anglers are on board, all concentrating their efforts on fluke while drifting with a bottom rig. Two additional outfits are rigged up. One outfit is rigged with live bait and drifted out to swim at intermediate depths. A second outfit is rigged with bait and fished near the surface, suspended by a plastic snap-float, so the bait drifts 4 or 5 feet beneath the surface.

The two outfits are placed out of the way in rod holders, with their drags set lightly and their clickers on. Basically, they're left unattended throughout the day. While admittedly not requiring any degree of skill, the dead-stick outfits invariably bring strikes. If you're within the range of the favorite four, seldom can you fish an entire day on which a dead stick won't let go with the clicker's banshee scream of a strike. The dead stick will often provide a wake-up call, alerting you to fish you never realized were present. If the dead stick is being fished on the bottom it'll catch you not only fluke but also sea bass, croaker, and weakfish, while the intermediate and top lines often get walloped by stripers, blues, Spanish mackerel, little tuna, and oceanic bonito, to name but a few. Thus, when the action for the targeted species is slow, it provides an opportunity to switch over and enjoy a day's action with other species.

While the dead-stick approach relates primarily to drift fishing with natural baits, veteran anglers often keep a rod close at hand and rigged with a leadhead or diamond jig. Working a jig through the water column as you drift along with baits often results in strikes from fish that might have ignored your other offerings.

Many boatmen have their craft equipped with LORAN or GPS and a color fishfinder, all of which can prove extremely useful. Many use the LORAN and GPS primarily for navigation, failing to realize the importance of utilizing the units in concert with the fishfinder once fish are located. In the excitement of catching fish, the location at which they were hooked is often ignored, making it very difficult to double back. It's important to immediately hit the recall button on the LORAN and GPS, noting the water depth and observing the screen of the fishfinder, which will immediately indicate whether it was a stray fish or a school, and whether there was a big concentration of forage at the spot.

This information should always be entered in a logbook, so you can have a permanent record for future reference. Other entries in the log should be the sea condition, wind direction, and speed and stage of the tide. On future trips this information will prove invaluable, for it enables you to selectively return to a spot when all the conditions are similar.

DRIFTING FOR FLUKE

From early May through late October the fluke is the darling of drift fishermen throughout its range. Anglers catch them from cartop boats in practically every river along the coast, while those with larger boats head to open waters and the ocean to score. Perhaps the greatest numbers of anglers seeking the flatfish are those who board the hundreds of half-day and all-day party boats that sail from almost every inlet.

Fluke bury themselves in sand and mud bottoms, often with just their eyes exposed, and leisurely wait for a meal to be swept within range. It may be a sand eel or spearing, or perhaps a crab, sand bug, or unsuspecting squid. When it's within range the fluke shoots from the bottom, engulfing it in an instant. Thus, fluke fishing is a natural for the drifting angler, who can present his bait over a wide range of bottoms, assisted by the current and wind that move him along.

Teenagers like Jennifer Basilio enjoy drifting for fluke: It's relaxing, you can enjoy the sunshine, and you almost always make a good catch.

The old adage "two is better than one" holds true when selecting a terminal rig for fluke. The high-low rig presents one hook on the bottom and another 18 to 24 inches off the bottom. You can purchase high-low rigs at most coastal tackle shops, or tie your own if you choose.

It's easy to tie your own rigs. Begin by tying a dropper loop in your line, approximately 18 to 24 inches from its terminal end. Slip a single size 3/0 or 4/0 Beak, Claw, or Wide Gap hook snelled to 16 inches of fluorocarbon leader material onto the dropper loop.

Then tie a small three-way swivel directly to the end of your line. Tie a piece of 30- to 36-inch-long fluorocarbon leader material to one eye of the swivel. Snell a pair of the same-sized hooks to the leader, separated by an inch or two. Snelled in this manner, the rig is ideal with strip bait: One hook holds the head of the strip, and the other is placed in the center of it. When a fluke strikes, it's usually hooked on the trailing hook.

Tie an 8-inch-long piece of monofilament, lighter than the test of the line you're using, to the remaining eye of the swivel, with a loop in the end of it onto which you can slip your sinker. Thus, if you snag the bottom, the sinker will break free and you won't lose the entire rig. Bank- or dipsey-style sinkers are favored, because they slide easily across the bottom as you're drifting. Keep an assortment of sizes ranging from 1/2 through 16 ounces in your kit; this will cover all sea conditions.

The bottom hook of the rig should be baited with strip bait, such as squid, fluke belly, sea robin, or dogfish. The high hook is perfect for combination bait consisting of a small strip of squid and live killie. If weakfish are in the area you can slip a single sandworm on the high hook.

Fluke usually reside on open bottoms consisting of sand or mud, which makes drifting for them easy. For best results try to keep your rig drifting nearly perpendicular. This may require using a heavy sinker, particularly when there's a strong wind blowing and a fast drift.

Quite often the best catches of the entire season are made during a howling nor'easter when the drift is so fast it requires a full 16 ounces to hold the bottom. Here, too, the successful angler is the one who always keeps his rig on the bottom. Too light a sinker will cause the rig to balloon off the bottom during a fast drift, and you just won't score.

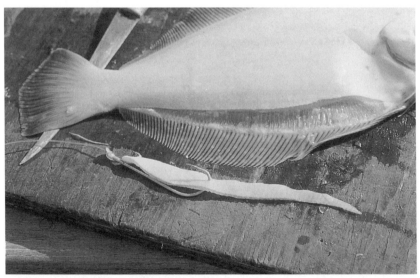

A properly cut strip bait from a fluke doesn't waste any meat, yet is very effective. Check local regulations before completing the final cleaning.

Drifting for fluke is fun for youngsters, as demonstrated here by a group who fished off Captree, Long Island. They were participants in the Children's Fishing Program sponsored by the New York Metropolitan Outdoor Press Association.

Aboard the party boats it's wise to arrive at the dock early. The bow and stern spots provide a decided advantage, because your line is never under the boat during a drift. Invariably the high-hook catches come from these two positions.

Cold currents will often put fluke off their feed. Just a couple of hours of a strong southeast wind on a summer afternoon often completely shuts down their feeding activity.

Small fluke are content to feed on the small forage found on open bottoms. The doormats weighing in at 5 pounds or more often take up residence along the perimeter of rock-strewn bottoms and mussel beds, for this bottom holds forage such as cunner, sea bass, tautog, ling, whiting, and crabs. Each season the biggest fluke are generally hooked from such spots. Unfortunately, there's also an attrition of terminal tackle as a result of snagging the bottom. This risk can be minimized by keeping your line as close to perpendicular as possible while you drift.

Early in the season as the fluke move inshore from the water of the continental shelf, and again in fall when they head back out, they'll often stop at the many lumps, banks, and ridges located several miles from the beach. Often there's a concentration of sand eels at such spots, and the fluke school up and feed heavily before moving on. Many of these spots are in water 50 to 60 feet deep, but provide superb action during the times when the fluke congregate.

DRIFTING FOR BLUEFISH

On the same lumps, banks, and ridges where you find fluke, you're apt to find bluefish as well. They visit the high bottom to feed on the herring, mackerel, squid, and other forage that's so plentiful.

Inshore bluefish move about a great deal, and most anglers have visions of them feeding on the surface, slashing bait and creating havoc. This isn't the case offshore, where they're often schooled and feeding at intermediate depths, and quite often right down on the bottom. They'll also take up residence around wrecks, with huge, tightly packed schools just above or off to the side of the wreck.

Drifting the high bottom and water adjacent to wrecks often provides exciting sport. A basic bottom rig is perfect for this fishing. Begin by tying a three-way swivel to your line. Tie a short piece of monofilament to one eye of the swivel with a loop onto which you can slip a bank-style sinker of sufficient weight to hold the bottom.

To the remaining eye of the swivel tie a piece of 40-pound-test leader material. Complete the rig by tying a long-shank Carlisle- or Beak-style hook, size 5/0 through 7/0. The long-shank hook style is preferred, because it prevents a bluefish from biting through the leader. If really big bluefish—those choppers in the 12- to 20-pound class—are present, many anglers employ a leader of No. 8 or 9 coffee-colored stainless steel, which prevents the blues from biting through the leader when they inhale a bait.

Chunk bait, measuring 1 inch in width by 3 inches in length and cut from a menhaden, herring, mackerel, or butterfish, makes ideal bait. Keep the rig on the bottom and just hold on; the strike of a bluefish is often very forceful, and in deep water provides an exciting challenge.

If the fishfinder shows blues in tightly packed schools at mid-depth, you can use the same rig; simply let it settle in the water column to the depth where the fish are schooled. When the blues are up near the surface, just tie a leader and hook directly to the end of your line and drift the chunk bait out as you drift along. During a fast drift the addition of a rubber-cored sinker will help keep the bait from getting too near the surface.

Don't hesitate to employ a diamond jig or leadhead jig to probe the depths as you drift along. Sometimes the blues will respond to these more readily than to natural bait, particularly when you use a speed retrieve.

DRIFTING FOR STRIPERS AND WEAKS

As has been noted in numerous chapters, the favorite four often cover a great deal of area during the course of a day. Sometimes your fishfinder will show a blank screen for hours on end; then suddenly, on the same grounds, the forage and bait appear as a dense cloud. This is particularly true with stripers and weaks, both of which often fall into a traveling regimen that can be tracked and used to advantage as you seek them.

It's doubtful there's a striper alive that would pass up an offering of one or two large Maine sandworms being drifted along enticingly on the bottom. The same might be said of weakfish, for sandworms annually account for many yellowfins.

A basic bottom rig consisting of a three-way swivel, a short length of monofilament with a sinker loop and dipsey sinker to one eye of the swivel, and a 36-inch-long fluorocarbon leader with a size 1/0 through 3/0 Claw-style hook with a baitholder shank is ideal.

Permit the sandworm to open its mouth, insert the hook, and run it out about an inch from its head. The baitholder shank of the hook will hold the worm in position so it won't slide down and bunch up. If the worm is small, add a second worm in much the same manner. Use sufficient sinker weight so that the rig just bounces the bottom as you drift along.

You can use this same rig with any of the live baits customarily used for stripers and weaks, adjusting for their larger size by using a larger hook without a baitholder shank.

It's often wise to have at least one rig that you can fish at an intermediate level, for sometimes the stripers and weakfish are up in the water column.

This is easily accomplished by tying a 3- to 4-foot-long fluorocarbon leader to your line using a surgeon's knot. Depending on the bait you plan to use, tie a size 3/0 through 6/0 Claw- or Beak-style hook to the leader. Attach a plastic snap-float to your line, positioning it so that the hook bait will be at the depth you desire. Finish off the rig by adding a small rubber-cored sinker to the leader, which will help keep the bait at the desired depth as you drift along.

With this rig you can bait with live sandworms, as just described, or you can use a live squid, herring, menhaden, mackerel, mullet, spot, croaker, eel, or other small forage fish.

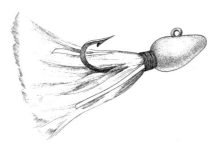

What will surprise you is how the fish will vary the depths at which they're feeding. Sometimes the bottom rigs bring consistent strikes, while on the very next tide the fish are up in the water column and only the baits on a float rig score. That's why it's important to consistently fish all levels of the water column while drifting. Don't hesitate to work a lure while others are fishing with natural baits. This combination is a technique that pays handsome dividends throughout the entire season.

Many anglers feel that if they had to select one lure for all applications it would have to be the leadhead jig. Available in a variety of sizes and shapes, with feather, hair, bucktail, or plastic skirt, it proves effective whether cast from boat or beach, trolled, or jigged.

While the contemplative allure of drift fishing may be its main attraction, in the final analysis it's the catching that really draws so many to this relaxing, fun-filled pastime while seeking the favorite four.

8

CHUMMING

No less an authority than *Webster's Dictionary* describes *chum* as "chopped fish, or the like, thrown overboard to attract fish." The definition is one of the shortest entries in the dictionary! In practice, there's a lot more to it than you'd expect from *Webster's*.

Tackle and Techniques

While it's relatively easy to do, there's a discipline attached to chumming. Tides, current, location, type of chum used, method of presenting the bait—all combine to separate the seasoned angler from the tyro. Indeed, many a novice has his first comeuppance when observing a neighboring angler catching fish nonstop while receiving nary a strike. It's the chum that makes the difference.

Striped bass, bluefish, weakfish, and fluke are all readily attracted to a chum line. It consists of an easy meal being dispensed, and they can satisfy their appetites without having to work for the meal. A wide range of techniques can be employed to chum these species within range of hook baits or lures worked through the chum slick. Throughout this chapter each will be discussed at length. While some are potent for one particular species, for the most part all of the favorite four will respond to them with minor modifications.

The key to success while chumming is maintaining a steady, uninterrupted flow of chum. Over time, experience will dictate the correct amount of chum to use: You want to attract the fish, not feed them. The single biggest mistake made by many newcomers is getting caught up in the excitement of catching fish, and in turn failing to maintain continuity of the chum slick. It's best to assign the chumming chores to one individual, trading off from time to time.

There may be times when you encounter moon tides, when the current is running very swiftly and the chum and bait settle, but the hook bait tends to be swept away and stays near the surface. On such occasions slip a small rubber-cored sinker onto your line 3 or 4 feet from the bait. Experiment with the weight of the sinker until your bait is in the strike zone. Often this little adjustment makes the difference between success and failure.

At other times you may experience little or no current, and while the chum is moving at mid-depths, your rig settles to the bottom. Then it's appropriate to add a very small rubber-cored sinker to help keep your line traveling perpendicularly to the bottom, and attach a float to the line to suspend the bait at the desired depth.

BOTTOM RIGS

On rare occasions, particularly when bluefish take up residence above a wreck, they'll stay deep, feeding on the chum chunks as they drift down and refusing to come to the surface. When this occurs, it's often evident, for you can read the fish on your electronics but have no activity or strikes with baits fished near the surface or at intermediate levels. Then it's best to switch. Employ a bottom rig to get right to the bottom or a couple of feet above it.

Begin by tying a small barrel swivel directly to the end of your line using a uni-knot. Next, to one of the swivel eyes tie a 30-inch-long piece of 30-pound-test fluorocarbon leader material, along with a 6- to 8-inch-long leader of No. 8 or 9 stainless steel. Tie an 8- to 10-inch long piece of leader material to the remaining eye of the swivel, and tie a large loop in the end of it, onto which to slip your sinker. Use a bank- or dipsey-style sinker. The sinker weight may range from an ounce or two to upward of 8 ounces, so that the line is held as near perpendicular to the bottom as possible.

A rig like this sent right to the bottom often brings fast action from fish that simply refuse to move away from the wreck, ridge, or lump on which they're residing.

You can also employ a leadhead jig with plastic bait tail, casting it out, letting it settle to the bottom, and then working it back with a jigging action. This causes the jig to dart ahead and up from the bottom then flutter back down, much like a struggling baitfish, often resulting in strikes from fluke resting on the bottom or moving up in the chum line.

HIGH-LOW RIG

A high-low bottom rig proves very effective while chumming for fluke. This rig keeps one hook down on the bottom and a second, or high hook, 18 to 24 inches above the bottom. An easy way to make up a high-low rig is to tie a surgeon's loop at the terminal end of your line to accommodate the sinker. A bank- or dipsey-style sinker is ideal, just heavy enough to hold the rig on the bottom.

Then tie a dropper loop 2 or 3 inches from the sinker loop, and another dropper loop 16 to 18 inches from the first.

Slip a snelled hook with a 24- to 36-inch-long leader onto the low dropper loop near the sinker, and a snelled hook with a 12- to 15-inch-long leader to the high dropper loop. When rigged in this manner, the current will pull the hook baits away from the line, and the short-leader high hook will flutter enticingly above the low hook on the rig.

There are two schools of thinking as to what is the most effective way of fishing the rig. Many anglers position their rig 5 to 20 feet down-current from the chum pot, intercepting fluke moving to the source of the chum. They leave the rig motionless on the bottom, with the bait appearing to stem the tide. Other anglers keep their line nearly per-pendicular to the bottom and gently raise and lower the rod tip, caus-ing the baits to lift off the bottom, flutter, and settle back down again.

Hook styles and sizes become a matter of personal choice. The long-shank Carlisle style is very popular, because the shank makes it rela-tively easy to remove the hook—an important consideration when releasing undersized fish. The Claw and Beak styles are also effective, as is the Wide Gap style and, more recently, the Circle hook.

There's a consensus these days that bigger is better in hook sizes, primarily because many of the fluke that are caught by recreational anglers are undersized and have to be released. This is a departure from the previous practice of using a small hook that could more eas-ily be ingested by a fluke and often resulted in deeply hooked fish that rarely survived.

Chumming for fluke is done primarily in bay and river waters, where the fluke average in the 1- to 4-pound class. Size 1/0 through 4/0 hooks are well suited to fish of this weight. In the case of Circle hooks, size 7/0 and 8/0 prove popular, and result in the majority of fluke being hooked in the corner of their jaw, which makes unhooking less difficult than with other styles.

Live mummichogs, popularly called killies or minnows along the coast, make effective bait when chumming. As the fluke pick up the tiny pieces of chum drifting across the bottom, a lively killie hooked through the lips quickly attracts their attention. They forgo the chum for the more substantial forage.

Spearing, sand eels, and mullet are also very effective hook baits. Live or dead shrimp can be used, too. A strip of squid proves effective, as does a strip bait cut from such species as sea robin, dogfish, or mackerel. Often the combination of live killie and strip bait proves deadly, because the movement of the killie gives an enhanced fluttering movement to the strip.

Chumming for Bluefish, Stripers, and Weaks

A prime consideration if you're going to chum is where you plan to fish. Each of the favorite four has different habits, and the greater your knowledge of their habits and movements, the easier it is for you to select a strategy.

Bluefish are readily attracted to a chum line, and of the favorite four have perhaps the most ravenous appetites and consume the greatest amount of food. There are times when a school of bluefish is spread over a wide range of bottoms, sometimes several miles in length. At other times they're tightly schooled up over a wreck, ridge, or high bottom lump. In each instance their location is most often determined by the availability of forage.

When the fish are spread over a large area, it becomes appropriate to drift with the wind or tide, dispensing chum as you go. The chum will attract the fish, which in turn will stay with the chum slick, often attracting additional fish as you move along.

When the fish are located tight to an area, such as a wreck, it's difficult to employ a drift. You may attract only a few fish as you drift over the school, and in a matter of minutes are far from the majority of fish. In this situation the best technique is to locate the wreck with fishfinding gear and note the schools of fish above it. It's often wise to

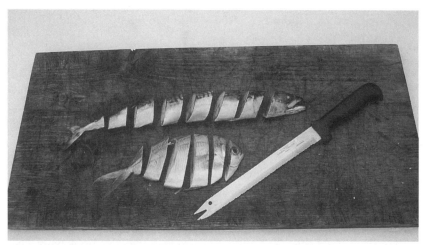

Boatmen who chum off Watch Hill, Rhode Island, use mackerel and butterfish chunks to chum bluefish within range.

drop a marker buoy. Then judge wind direction and tidal flow, and anchor so that your boat is positioned where the current will carry the chum to the schooled fish and attract them to your hook baits.

Bluefish will respond to a wide variety of fish as chum. By far the most popular method is to use a combination of ground fish and chunks of fish. The chum of choice is fresh-ground menhaden, popularly called mossbunker. When freshly ground isn't available, frozen chum may be used, although many anglers consider the fresh to be far more effective. Menhaden chum is extremely oily and establishes a good slick as it's ladled overboard. When menhaden aren't available, herring, mackerel, and butterfish are good substitutes. Ground chum has a thick consistency, so it's best to mix it with seawater, resulting in a soup that can easily be dispensed with a ladle.

Menhaden, herring, mackerel, or butterfish should be cut into pieces 1/2 inch wide by 2 inches long or thereabouts. A serrated knife makes the job easy, as it readily cuts through the bony fish.

Once positioned, either at anchor or drifting, chumming begins by tossing out a ladle of diluted ground chum and five or six pieces of the chunks, so they drift off together. As the chum drifts from sight, 25 or 30 feet from the boat, repeat the step, tossing additional ground chum and chunks overboard.

Bluefish caught while chumming provides exciting sport, and a light- to medium-weight outfit is more than adequate. Although many anglers use spinning tackle, the multiplying or conventional reel provides better control and is the reel of choice for most anglers. A rod rated for 12- to 20-pound-test line, measuring 6 1/2 to 7 feet in overall length, is ideal. A reel with a capacity of 150 to 200 yards of 15- or 20-pound-test monofilament line is more than adequate.

When rigging terminal tackle, just tie a long-shank Beak- or Claw-style hook directly to the end of your line and you're ready to go. The only problem is that when big bluefish take the bait, they'll often inhale it deep, and this enables them to bite through the mono. As insurance against bite-offs, many anglers tie a small black barrel swivel to the end of their line, followed by a 6- to 8-inch-long leader of No. 8 or 9 stainless-steel wire, followed by the hook.

The hook size should be tailored to the size of the fish encountered. Because bluefish are schooling fish, the majority of a catch is generally the same size. With 2- to 4-pounders, a size 2/0 or 3/0 Claw or Beak style is fine; move up to a 4/0 through 5/0 when the fish are in the 5- to 10-pound range, and a 7/0 should serve you well when the majority of fish encountered are in the 10- to 15-pound range and larger.

If there's a swift current running, add a rubber-cored sinker to your line, which will take your bait to the depth at which the chum is drifting.

For hook bait employ pieces of the fish you're using as chunks. Bait cut from the back section of menhaden, mackerel, or butterfish is ideal, because it's firm meat that isn't easily ripped from the hook. Run the hook through the skin on one side, and bring it out the other, so the point and barb of the hook are exposed and in position to quickly penetrate as a fish inhales the bait.

There are occasions when bluefish refuse chunk baits. Using small whole butterfish, spearing, sand eels, or mullet as hook baits should quickly bring strikes.

Under normal conditions, while drifting or anchored with moderate current, ease the bait into the water and permit it to flow with the current and the chum. The key is keeping the bait moving in a natural manner. As bluefish move up the slick, aroused by the scent of the ground chum and picking up the small number of chunks drifting along, they'll see your bait drifting at the same level and the same speed as the other chunks and swim right up and inhale it.

After paying out 75 to 100 feet of line, lock the reel into gear, reel in the bait, and begin paying it out again. The key is keeping the bait drifting along naturally. If you just let it out, lock the reel into gear, and permit it to hang in the current, the bait will spin in an unnatural manner and be swept toward the surface, minimizing your chances of receiving a strike.

Inasmuch as you're maintaining minimal thumb pressure on the line as it pays out from the reel, you've got to be alert at all times. Suddenly the line will begin to move off at a rapid pace as a fish picks up the bait and turns to swim away. Always keep your rod tip pointed in the direction the line is moving. As a fish moves off, permit it to take several feet of line, all the while maintaining light pressure on the reel spool to prevent an overrun. Then lock the reel into gear, lift back smartly to set the hook, and hold on!

Once the hook strikes home, a bluefish will peel line from the reel. This is where it's important to have a moderately set drag, so the fish can take line without it breaking—which might occur if too much drag pressure is exerted. Remember, you're using light- to medium-weight tackle to enjoy maximum sport, and a heavy drag setting just isn't compatible.

After the first or second run of the fish, or even more if it's a heavy-weight, the fish will begin to tire, and you can exert additional pressure by systematically pumping the fish from the depths. Use long, smooth strokes with the rod, gaining line as you lower the rod tip.

Never yank or jerk back with the rod; this will often result in a line break or rip the hook from the fish's jaw.

When brought alongside the boat, smaller fish are easily swung aboard. Those that appear to be 8 pounds or more are better gaffed than lifted. Once aboard, make certain to take great care when unhooking all bluefish, because their sharp teeth can inflict serious injury if you're not cautious. Use a long-nosed plier or dehooker if the fish is hooked deep, or, better still, cut the leader and remove the hook and leader later. It's easier to tie on another rig than to suffer injury.

Weakfish and stripers are often attracted to surface noises, such as those emitted by small forage species swimming near the surface. This has resulted in many anglers employing a popping cork float rigged 4 or 5 feet ahead of the hook bait. The float's concave head, when drawn through the water by twitching your rod tip, emits a popping or gurgling sound. This attracts the attention of fish moving up the chum line, which spot the shrimp drifting just beneath the float and often inhale it in an instant.

Chumming with grass shrimp works both day and night and is an extremely effective technique. On a typical day it's not unusual to catch all of the favorite four, for often fluke will move off the bottom to seize the free-drifting shrimp. Bluefish will inhale the shrimp too; they aren't averse to anything in sight that's edible.

Striped bass are known to relish feeding on clams. When coastal storms uncover clam beds and the crashing waves break open and expose clams, the linesiders have a feast. The use of clam meat as chum has grown in popularity lately, especially the clam bellies that are available from many clam processors located along the coast.

The key when chumming with clam bellies is to do so in an area frequented by stripers, and at a time when the current is moving at a moderate speed.

Most often stripers will take up stations to feed around bridge abutments and icebreakers. They'll generally avoid feeding when the current is swift at midtide, preferring times when the water is moving at a moderate rate of speed and they can expend little energy. Just before and after slack water the fish feed aggressively, and you've got to be anchored and in position to take advantage of that short period when feeding activity is at its peak.

Unlike bluefish, which feed aggressively and when full can be observed disgorging food only to then begin feeding again, striped bass stop feeding once they've filled their stomachs. Because of this you've got to be especially careful when chumming with clam bellies, for if you chum too heavily the bass will simply gorge on the chum and stop feeding.

Clam bellies are messy to deal with. They come in frozen blocks, and the thawing juices can make decks slippery. A good practice is to permit the bellies to begin thawing before you head out on the water. As they soften, use a serrated knife to slice through the block, which cuts the bellies into smaller pieces instead of big globs. Using a soup ladle, you can then ladle the chum overboard sparingly, teasing the stripers to feed on it, and enhancing your chances by not having them fill up on the chum. A pull-type crap trap filled with clam bellies, tied shut, weighted, and lowered to the bottom makes an effective chum pot.

Employ much the same technique as described earlier for chumming for bluefish. You'll encounter much the same situation in coastal rivers, with swift-flowing water requiring the addition of a rubber-cored sinker. At slack tide, when there's practically no movement, a float is essential.

There are also times when a bottom rig brings good results on a running tide. At such times the stripers will be in an eddy, waiting for the clam chum to be carried to them. A bottom rig, such as described earlier, with the addition of a cork float on the leader keeps the rig on the bottom, yet the cork suspends the clam belly bait a foot or two off the bottom, where the movement of the current causes the membrane to flutter enticingly.

Chumming for Fluke

It's common practice to chum for stripers, blues, and weaks using the techniques just described. As noted, on regular occasions fluke wander into the slick. For the most part, however, there's but limited chumming activity specifically targeting the summer flatfish.

Anglers who are successful chumming for summer flounder use much the same technique as is employed to coax winter flounder into range during the cold-weather months. Because flatfish primarily frequent the bottom, you've got to get the chum down deep and fish your baits right on the bottom. To do so a chum pot is employed.

Chum pots are available at most coastal tackle shops. Approximately 4 to 5 inches in diameter, with a 1/4-inch-thick lead bottom, the pot has sides of 1/4-inch galvanized mesh screening and a hinged top.

Freshly ground chum flows from the pot very quickly and often results in overfeeding the fish. Because of this, many anglers insert frozen logs of chum into the pot. As they thaw while resting on the bottom, the chum oozes from the pot at a moderate rate of speed.

GRIND-YOUR-OWN FLUKE CHUM

Many anglers grind their own chum. Using a coarse grinder will result in pieces of chum approximately 1/8 inch in diameter—sufficiently small to exit through the mesh of the chum pot. The tiny pieces of chum are big enough to tempt a fluke to seek their source and move within range of hook baits fished on the bottom nearby.

Squid is a favorite chum, although spearing, sand eels, and killies may all be ground into pieces. Some anglers grind up small menhaden, which are oily and establish a slick in addition to the pieces drifting along the bottom. Ground clams are also effective.

After it's ground, place the chum mixture in paper cups of a size that will fit into the chum pot, then freeze the cups. On the day you plan to use them, keep the frozen logs in an ice chest until you're ready to insert one into the chum pot.

On reaching the fishing grounds, double-anchor to keep your boat in position right over the chum pot. Tear off the paper cup and insert a frozen chum log into the chum pot. Lower it to the bottom using a piece of nylon cord. As the chum pot rests on the bottom, periodically give the cord a good yank, lifting it from the bottom and permitting the chum to ooze from the pot and travel with the current along the bottom.

Grass Shrimp

Weakfish and stripers that set up residence in bays and rivers often feed extensively on the grass shrimp that are so plentiful in these waterways. They cruise around bridge pilings, piers, bulkheads, and marsh grass where the shrimp seek sanctuary or cling to the structure. Often the shrimp are swept along with the current, and the weaks and bass just gorge on them.

Grass shrimp make excellent chum and can be purchased live from bait purveyors along the coast. Many anglers choose to net their own chum using a seine or fine-meshed, handheld dip net worked along the pilings. While live grass shrimp are preferred, freshly frozen shrimp also work very well.

Chumming with grass shrimp is best accomplished by anchoring in a waterway known to harbor weakfish and stripers. There should be a moderate current to carry the chum and keep it from settling to the bottom, but not so swift as to cause the fish to exert excess energy in order to feed.

The ideal situation is to fish in the many barrier island bays separating the mainland from the islands, as are found off Long Island, New Jersey, Virginia, and the Carolinas. Most of the bay waters have marsh grass banks or are bulkheaded and range in depth to no more than 6 or 8 feet for the most part.

The key is anchoring so that your boat doesn't swing with the tide or wind. This calls for a pair of anchors, one at the bow and another at the stern, which securely holds your boat in one position. Thus, as the grass shrimp is dispensed overboard, it drifts at the mercy of the current and the fish are attracted directly to your hook baits.

Most anglers who chum with grass shrimp use a very light outfit; a one-handed spinning outfit rated for 10-pound-test line or a comparable conventional outfit is ideal. Stick with rods measuring 5 to 6 feet in overall length.

Because small bluefish often wander into the slick, many anglers like to employ a leader heavier than their 10-pound-test line, to avoid their biting through the line if the hook is tied directly to the line. Use a 3- or 4-foot-long piece of 15-pound-test fluorocarbon leader material, and tie it to the terminal end of the line using a surgeon's knot. The refractive index of the leader is such that it is virtually invisible in the water, which helps increase the number of strikes you receive in the clear inshore waters.

A Beak- or Claw-style hook with a baitholder shank is perfect for this fishing. The baitholder shank has two sharp barbs, which hold shrimp securely as you impale three or four of them on your hook.

Live grass shrimp are a favorite chum when seeking weakfish in Peconic Bay, Long Island, New York.

Keep the hooks on the small side; you don't want the weight and size of the hook to cause the hook baits to settle too deeply. A 1 or 2, or a 1/0 or 2/0, is about as large as you'll want to go.

As with all chumming, do it sparingly, because if you chum too heavily with grass shrimp the fish will hold well back in the chum line and not move up to within range of your hook baits. Toss out five or six shrimp at a time, giving them time to drift away before dispensing more.

Usually you'll be able to drift your shrimp bait out, and the current will carry it nicely with the chum. There are times, however, that even in the quiet reaches of coastal bays and sounds you'll experience the same situation encountered while offshore chumming for bluefish: Sometimes the hook bait will sink to the bottom, while at other times the current will carry it swiftly near the surface. Use a small rubber-cored sinker to send it to a desired level, and a plastic or cork float to keep it near the surface.

Chumming requires patience and knowing the water you plan to fish, the bottom conformation, and where the favorite four take up stations to feed at various stages of the tide. Still, once you master this technique of coaxing fish to bait drifted out with the chum, you'll find it extremely rewarding, particularly if light-tackle fishing is your forte.

Fresh clams are one of the most popular striped bass baits and are most effective fished right on the bottom in areas known to harbor stripers.

9

BOTTOM FISHING

Throughout this book there are many references to the movement of striped bass, bluefish, weakfish, and fluke. Trollers cover miles of water as they seek them out, as do drift fishermen. The bottom fisherman takes a different tack. He anchors at spots where the favorite four are known to frequent, fishes his baits on the bottom—and in between, too—and waits for the fish to come to him.

Tackle and Techniques

Currents carry forage of all kinds. The stronger the current, the more small baitfish try to get out of it, often taking up stations in the quiet water adjacent to rips and in eddies. The swirling whirlpools also hold crabs and shrimp, a smorgasbord feast. By anchoring just off such spots, you can cast or drift your baited bottom rig into the swirling current, content with the knowledge that fish are certain to move through.

Fish often position themselves ahead of or behind bridge abutments, for here, too, the current has a dead spot where the fish can wait for a meal without expending energy fighting the current.

Channel edges are another location that fish traverse as they move from spot to spot. Wherever two bodies of water meet, such as two rivers funneling into a single river, there is a clashing of currents, and here, too, the fish will congregate, for an easy meal is often available.

The key in such locations is properly anchoring your boat. The anchor should be dropped well up from the rocky bottom, bridge abutment, or eddy. One anchor will usually suffice, but if wind and current cause the boat to swing excessively, a second anchor is recommended; it will hold you steady in one position.

It then becomes a waiting game. Patience is the key, for often a choice location will seem devoid of fish for hours. Then suddenly stripers or weaks will move in, sometimes singles, pods of half a dozen fish, or virtually stacked like cordwood. Often this occurs just before or after slack water, and the fishing is fast and furious, only to turn off as quickly as it turned on.

While stripers, weaks, and fluke are most often hugging the bottom as they take up stations in a rip or eddy, there are often times when they'll move up in the water column as the current slows before slack water. While this chapter is devoted to bottom fishing, it's always wise to dead-stick an outfit, with a single bait drifted out in the current, using just a small rubber-cored sinker (or no sinker at all) and permitting a squid, sandworm, or live bait to flutter in the current at intermediate levels. This is the bait that will often bring strikes from bluefish.

FLOATING JIGHEAD

A rig that has long been popular with freshwater fisherman, but only in recent years has grown in popularity with saltwater anglers, is the floating jighead. It consists of a jig hook, with the eye turned up, and a Styrofoam or cork body cemented to the hook, usually a Beak style with a baitholder shank. Hook and head sizes vary from 2 through 3/0. The oblong body is painted like a fish's head; the favored body colors include white, yellow, and hot pink, with painted eyes.

The favored method of rigging the floating jighead is to tie it to a 30- to 36-inch-long piece of 20-pound-test fluorocarbon leader material, which in turn is attached to a small three-way swivel. A short piece of monofilament is tied to one eye of the swivel, with a surgeon's loop at the end. Slipping a dipsey-style sinker onto the loop completes the rig, which is then tied to your line.

The favorite bait for use with the floating jighead is a large sandworm. By waiting until the sandworm opens its mouth, you can easily slip in the point of the hook and then bring it out about an inch from the head, the baitholder shank holding it securely in place.

When this rig is placed in the water, the sinker settles to the bottom while the floating jighead suspends the bait off the bottom—anywhere from 1 to 3 feet, depending on the flow of the current. The current pushing against the jighead causes it to move about, slipping and sliding, with the trailing live sandworm swimming enticingly, much as if it weren't on a hook.

Another advantage is that the sandworm is well up from the bottom, usually out of range of crabs.

You can also use bloodworms, strips of squid, or the head and tentacles of a squid with the floating jighead.

This rig is especially productive when fished in locations where fish congregate to avoid swift currents and stem the tide as they wait for food to be swept their way. Stripers and weakfish will often take up stations where there is a high spot or rocky bottom, positioning themselves ahead of or behind the spot where the current moderates as it passes around it.

Bob Rosko unhooks a weakfish for daughter Kristine, who hooked it on a high-low bottom rig, with a strip bait on the bottom and a sandworm on top.

HIGH-LOW RIG

The high-low rig has historically been the favorite choice of bottom fishermen, for it presents a pair of baits to the fish, one directly on the bottom and a second 18 to 24 inches off it. Many tackle shops stock ready-made high-low rigs, or you can easily make up your own.

A rig can be made by tying a pair of dropper loops directly into your line's terminal end, spacing them an appropriate distance apart, and then finishing off with a surgeon's loop at the terminal end onto which you slip your sinker. This method of making up the rig is fine if you're using 20-pound-test or heavier line. It's not recommended if your lines are lighter than this, because the rig is often subjected to abrasion on the bottom, which could result in a line break.

If you're using 10- or 12-pound test it's best to make up a rig using 20-pound-test fluorocarbon leader material. Begin with a 36-inch-long piece and tie a tiny barrel swivel to the end, onto which you'll tie your line. Then tie in the pair of dropper loops and finish off with a surgeon's loop to hold the sinker.

To the dropper loops attach a pair of snelled hooks on 18-inch leaders, slip a bank- or dipsey-style sinker on the end loop, and you're ready to bait up.

The Beak, Claw, and Live Bait hook styles are the most popular, with sizes ranging from 1/0 through 5/0 suitable for most bottom-fishing situations targeting the favorite four. To prevent injuring fish that have to be released, many anglers now employ barbless Beak hooks, which prevent injury to the fish's jaw and gills.

FISHFINDER RIG

A fishfinder rig is little more than a hard plastic loop with a sinker snap at the other end. The line is passed through the loop, which permits the rig to slide on the line, after which a small barrel swivel, leader, and hook are attached. The fishfinder was originally designed to enable a fish to pick up the bait and move off with it, without feeling any resistance from the weight of the sinker. Experience shows that most fish simply inhale the bait and really don't move off with it until it's well into their mouths. The rig continues to be popular with bottom fishermen and can be used with all of the popular bottom baits, including squid, clams, seaworms, chunk baits, and live baitfish.

Types of Bait

Throughout some sections of the Northeast the striped bass is nicknamed squidhound, because it relishes squid. Surprisingly, most anglers who use squid for bait cut the long, tubular body of the squid into strips and discard the head. This head section, however—with its big eyes and tentacles hanging loosely—is an attractive bait. Using the high-low rig, slip the hook lightly through the head of each bait, so that the current pushing against the baits causes them to flutter enticingly. It's not unusual to catch two or three of the favorite four during a single day's leisurely bottom-fishing outing.

Each season some of the largest of the favorite four are caught on chunk baits fished on the bottom. Always remember that fish have to be constantly moving and searching for a meal. They'll seldom pass up any food. What makes chunk bait especially attractive is that it emits a scent that's carried with the current, attracting the fish to its source.

A very effective way of presenting a chunk bait is to use a bottom rig consisting of a three-way swivel, a short length of line to the sinker, and a 30- to 36-inch-long fluorocarbon leader with treble or Beak-style hook. Attach a small cork or Styrofoam float to the leader so that the bait is suspended off the bottom. With the current pushing against the float and bait, the bait hangs suspended and moving about. A hungry striper or blues just swims up and inhales it effortlessly.

A fresh menhaden is an excellent choice of chunk bait, because it's oily and the oil actually oozes from the bait when it's in the water. There are many opinions as to which chunks are the best to use—the head, body, or tail sections. The head, when cut from the body at a 45-degree angle, leaving some meat on it, is an excellent bait, as it con-

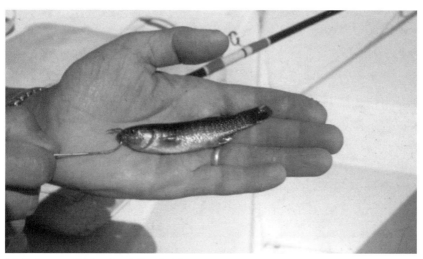

While bottom fishing, hook live baitfish like this mummichog—often called a minnow or killie—through the lips, enabling them to swim unimpeded in the current.

sists primarily of hard bone. This prevents it from washing out, and crabs can't easily rip it from the hook.

Mackerel, herring, spot, mullet, and almost any forage species may be effectively used as chunk bait. Fresh baits are preferred, although frozen baits regularly account for good catches.

If you're using a treble hook, place one of the hooks through the lips or nose of the bait, which leaves the remaining two hooks in a position to quickly penetrate. Many anglers prefer a Circle-style hook with big chunk bait; this hooks the fish in the corner of the mouth, making unhooking and release easier. Keep in mind that if you're using a Circle hook it's best to move up to size 12/0 or 14/0 for the same big bait that might otherwise be accommodated with a 6/0 or 7/0 Beak-style hook.

Bottom fishing is just one of many effective methods that can be employed to score with the favorite four. It requires patience—but, more important, also requires knowledge of the waters you plan to fish. Experience is gained through being alert to how wind and tide affect the water you plan to fish. The bottom fisherman waits for the fish to come to him, so being anchored where traveling fish can intercept the baits becomes paramount with this very effective technique.

The shallow reaches of coastal bays hold a large population of fluke throughout the summer, where anglers fishing from small boats enjoy many fine catches.

HOOKS FOR THE BIG FOUR

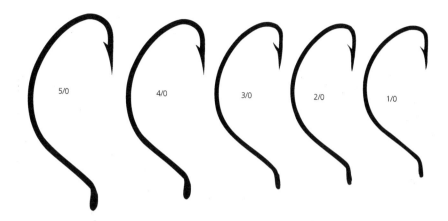

WIDE GAP HOOK

The fine-wire Wide Gap hook has excellent hooking and holding qualities.
It's especially effective when used with a strip bait or combination strip and
live killie, for fluke and weakfish.

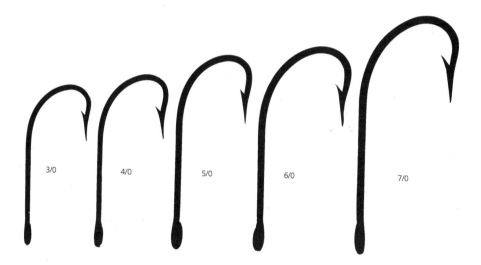

O'SHAUGHNESSY HOOK

The O'Shaughnessy-style hook is perhaps the most popular saltwater hook
of all. It's used primarily as a component of lures, such as metal squids,
leadhead jigs, and spoons. Many anglers also use this style with live baitfish
such as menhaden and herring.

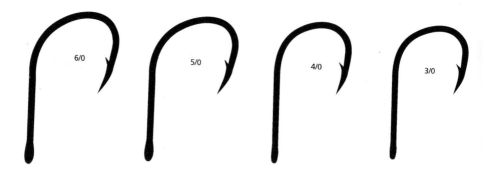

LIVE BAIT HOOK

The Live Bait–style hook, as its name implies, is designed for use with live baits such as herring, menhaden, mullet, and spot. It's a ringed hook with a short-shank, angled needle point, slightly kirbed. It's available in a tinned or black nickel finish.

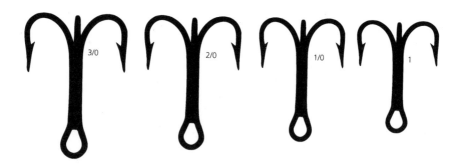

TREBLE HOOK

The most common application for a treble-style hook is with the wide variety of plugs. They're occasionally used on jigs, metal squids, and spoons, although single hooks are preferred for ease in unhooking. A treble can also be used effectively with live baits, securing the baitfish on but one of the hooks, leaving two exposed to penetrate.

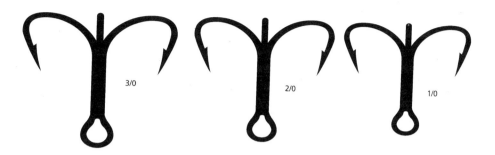

TRIPLE GRIP TREBLE HOOK

The Triple Grip style is the greatest advancement in treble hooks in many years. The hook's wide gap is the same size as a comparable standard treble. Its in-line hook eye and point create powerful hook sets at the time of the strike. Its unique bend forces the hooked fish into the elbow, making it virtually impossible to throw the hook. I regularly bend down the barbs, which facilitates unhooking and releasing fish unharmed.

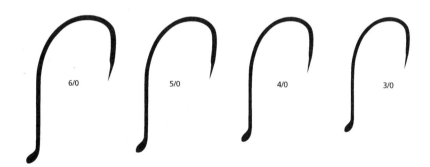

BARBLESS BEAK HOOK

The barbless Beak-style hook has grown in popularity as a result of the minimum size limits imposed on many species. The hooking and holding qualities of this hook are excellent. This style is especially popular with weakfish and fluke anglers, because it's removed with ease, with no damage to the fish's sensitive gills. To prevent a bait from slipping off the hook, many anglers, after placing the bait on the hook, slip on a 1/4-inch-square piece of rubber band, which clings to the hook.

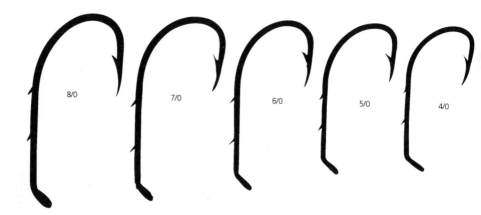

BEAK BAITHOLDER HOOK

The Beak-style hook with baitholder shank is very popular with bait fishermen. The two barbs on its shank hold the bait securely in place and prevent it from sliding into the bend of the hook. A single sandworm hangs straight, four or five grass shrimp are held securely, and a clam is held well up on the shank.

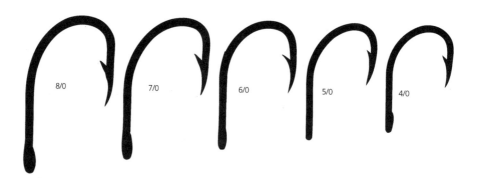

BEAK OR CLAW HOOK

The Beak- or Claw-style hook is a universally favored bait hook. It's available in long-shank or short-shank models. Pictured here are short-shank ringed models; the style is also available in turned-down or turned-up eye. The hook is forged and available in bronzed, gold-plated, and nickel-plated finishes.

14/0   13/0   12/0

CIRCLE HOOK

The Circle-style hook dates back centuries. Its unusual circle shape and the placement of the hook point and barb result in fish being hooked in the corner of the mouth. This makes removal and release of fish relatively easy, and has resulted in an expanded use of the hooks for striped bass and weakfish. Note that the hook sizes used are much larger than with regular J-style hooks.

A live menhaden coaxed a strike from the striper being brought aboard Captain John Capuano's Shinnecock Star.

10

NATURAL BAITS

The variety of natural baits found throughout the range of the striped bass, bluefish, weakfish, and fluke is staggering. It would be difficult to assign a number and equally difficult to determine just which baits are best for a particular species. Over a period of many years anglers often fall into a pattern of using specific bait out of habit. Sometimes it's a matter of availability, other times a matter of cost. For example, when moon tides or storms prevent the digging of sandworms in Maine, they're just not available. At other times they're available but their cost is so prohibitive that anglers shy away from using them.

It's important to recognize that the species discussed herein must feed regularly to survive. Most often they feed extensively on the forage that's most readily available, and as a general rule you'll be most successful using that bait. This doesn't necessarily mean that when menhaden are available in an area, they're the only food the fish will feed on.

Over the years boat anglers have developed patterns in their fishing, assuming that a given bait is the key to success—for example, being convinced that chunks of butterfish are superior to clams for bluefish. While this is generally true, a school of bluefish eager to feed will take any forage within range. Indeed, a bluefish will regularly take a clam bait, simply because clams are readily available.

The same holds true with fluke. Few anglers ever use sand bugs, grass shrimp, and crabs as bait for fluke, yet they constitute a major portion of the fish's diet. Killies or squid are more readily available for bait; hence they've become the norm.

Perhaps more important than a specific bait is its freshness and the manner in which you present it. Presentation is the key to success: The natural bait should be presented to a fish searching for a meal in the most lifelike manner possible.

Live Baits and the Big Four

Elsewhere in this book a variety of baits, rigs, and methods of presentation for shore-based anglers are discussed. They differ from the way boat fishermen present their bait in that from shore the bait is usually cast, while from a boat it's most often drifted astern, fished at intermediate depths or right on the bottom, and on occasion cast.

Boatmen are at a distinct advantage when it comes to using live baits. Many small boats have built-in live wells, enabling you to have live baitfish readily available on the fishing grounds. Local marinas and bait shops regularly stock live eels, killies, and menhaden, without question the three most popular and readily available live baitfish.

The key with using a live-bait well is providing aerated water so the baits have adequate oxygen and stay alive. Some boats have the live well built into the cockpit's sole, where water enters the bait compartment via a grille in the hull of the boat. Others have a circulating pump, pump-

The Atlantic coast's best-known live-bait angler is Al Wutkowski, shown here dipping herring from his holding pen prior to a trip to the fishing grounds.

ing seawater into the live well. Circular wells are necessary for most baitfish, which enable the fish to swim around and around. With a square well, some species swim into the corners and succumb as a result.

If you don't do a lot of live-bait fishing, you can purchase a portable live well. When used with oxygen tablets, this works very nicely for a limited number of live baits.

Other live bait is available right on the fishing grounds, and with a little effort can often be easily obtained. In fact, it's often fun catching bait on a light rod and reel, sometimes right at the dock before you leave for the fishing grounds. The spot—popularly called the Lafayette —is a very plentiful baitfish throughout the range of the favorite four. Spot are bottom feeders, and by using a high-low rig with size 6 or 8 Beak hooks and a small piece of clam or squid you can fill your bait well quickly. The croaker is another species that's easily caught and make a fine live bait for stripers, blues, and weakfish. Cunner, popularly called bergalls, are available around almost any submerged rock pile and easily caught with the same rig. The porgy is still another readily available bottom feeder and an excellent baitfish. Make certain to always adhere to the size and bag limit restrictions of the state you're in when obtaining baitfish for your live well.

During the summer months snapper bluefish ranging in size from 4 to 8 inches are available around most docks; they can be caught using a light outfit, a size 8 long-shank Carlisle hook with a plastic float rig, and spearing bait. Also around the docks are small jack crevalle, blue runners, and tinker mackerel, all of which are fine live baits.

On the fishing grounds live herring, Atlantic mackerel, and hickory shad may be caught using a diamond jig with two or three shad darts or teasers rigged ahead of it.

Schools of menhaden are often observed on the surface on fishing grounds, with schools of stripers, blues, and weaks beneath them. Bunkers won't take a lure, but you can catch them by casting a weighted treble hook beyond the schooling fish and retrieving it with a jigging motion, which will snag the fish.

Still another way to snag bunker is to make up a rig for that specific purpose. Use a 36-inch-long piece of 30-pound-test monofilament, and at 1-foot intervals tie in small treble hooks using a dropper loop. Pull the loop up tight so the treble is held firmly and doesn't swing freely on the loop. Attach a duolock snap at one end and a small black swivel at the other.

Use a small diamond jig or leadhead for casting weight. Cast the rig beyond the surfaced school of menhaden and permit it to settle somewhat. Begin your retrieve by smartly lifting the rod tip, causing the small trebles to be dragged across the back of the menhaden and impaling them.

Mention of live baits makes most of us immediately think of live fish, but there are many other kinds of live bait that can be used for the favorite four. When stripers and bluefish are feeding at night on live squid, it can be deadly bait. You can often use a dip net and scoop live squid from the water when they're attracted to the quartz lights as you drift along. Hook them lightly though the head, which will permit them to swim about enticingly, trailing their tentacles.

Joe Colabella uses a dip net to remove a live mackerel from a circular live well aboard his boat. Hooked lightly just ahead of the dorsal fin, mackerel are fine striped bass bait.

Blue crabs and calico crabs are also effective bait for the favorite four. While hard crabs may be used, a crab in the shedder or soft stage is best. A small- or medium-sized crab used whole is preferred, and should be held secure to the hook using elastic thread.

Seaworms, including sandworms, bloodworms, and tapeworms, are all fine live baits. Sandworms and bloodworms can be hooked through the mouth using a Beak-style hook with a baitholder shank. This results in the worm hanging freely and moving with the current. Tapeworms tend to break apart easily. They're best threaded onto the hook, with part of the worm hanging freely.

Hook Baits

Admittedly, it takes patience to obtain, keep alive, and fish with live baitfish. An option is to use dead baits, preferably fresh, although frozen baits annually account for many of the favorite four.

Some forage fish such as sand eels, mullet, spearing, herring, and rainfish are difficult to keep alive. All are fine hook baits. Best results are obtained by using a long-shank Carlisle-style hook. Run the hook in the bait's mouth and out its gills, then run it through the bait's midsection. When hooked in this manner and fished on the bottom or drifted, the bait won't spin; as a fish inhales it, the hook is in position to quickly penetrate.

Fresh or frozen squid are easily obtained and make fine hook baits. Squid can be cut into strips, and are extremely effective fluke and weakfish bait, especially when fished in combination with a live killie. The live baitfish swimming about keeps the squid strip fluttering, and readily draws strikes.

Striped bass devotees nicknamed it squidhound many years ago, although you seldom hear the species called such today. It's because the linesiders gorge on the abundant supply of this 10-armed cephalopod. Surprisingly, few anglers employ squid for stripers, yet those who do use whole squid score with fine catches. Hook one lightly through the head. Its dangling head and arms make it an attractive bait, fluttering in the current like a live squid.

Clams are regularly employed by surf and jetty fishermen to catch stripers. Surf clams are churned up by incoming waves, particularly during bad storms, exposing and breaking the clams. Bass gorge on them, and surf fishermen can easily cast their rigs to where the bass are feeding. Surprisingly, boat fishermen don't use the bivalves nearly as often. An angler who anchors offshore from bars paralleling the beach and casts clam- and squid-baited rigs toward shore will often register fine catches. This is particularly true after a storm when the bass are actively feeding. Sometimes the water is so discolored that you'd hardly think the fish could find the bait, yet through the scent of the clams resting on the bottom they zero in.

CHUNK, STRIP, AND OTHER BAITS

The live baits discussed earlier are also effective as chunk baits. When fish are hungry and feeding aggressively they may prefer a big, lively menhaden, mackerel, or herring. What they won't do is pass up a chunk of the same bait, drifted back in the current, suspended at intermediate levels via a plastic snap-float, or fished on the bottom with a sinker rig.

Butterfish are still another favored bait. They're firm and stay on the hook better than oily menhaden or soft mackerel.

A cutting board, razor-sharp filleting knife, and diamond knife sharpener are tools of the trade for devotees who use chunk baits and strip baits. Nothing will mangle bait quicker than a dull knife. Take the pain to have these important tools on board, and you can carefully cut chunk baits and strips from fresh or frozen fish and squid.

Several chunk baits can be cut from a single baitfish. Beginning just behind the head, cut diagonally at 1/2- to 1-inch intervals, which will result in several baits from each fish. Many anglers prefer using the head section of the bait. Place the hook through the lips. The bony structure of the head is less apt to wash away or soften in the water, and is not stripped from the hook by crabs as quickly as the fleshy part of the bait.

Often on the fishing grounds you'll catch species such as sea robins, dogfish, and cunner, which aren't highly regarded as table fish. All make fine strip baits when filleted and cut into long, thin strips, however.

Strip baits may also be cut from a fluke, without wasting any meat. Using a sharp filleting knife, make a cut the length of the fluke, paralleling the outline of the fish and 1/2 to 1 inch wide. This strip is muscle tissue adjoining the fins, and doesn't waste the nearby fillet. Two strips can be cut from the brown side of the fluke and two from the white side. Once cut from the fish, the strips may be trimmed to the desired size and make an excellent bait for weakfish and fish.

Take care not to cut the strips too wide. When you place a hook into the strip, position it near the strip's head so that as the hook lies over it doesn't burrow into the strip; it's always in a position to penetrate. Be careful to check local regulations with regard to using strip baits cut from fish covered by size limits. Most state laws require that if you cut a strip from a fish, you don't completely clean that fish until you return to shore.

Strip baits fished from a high-low rig, with one directly on the bottom off a three-way swivel and the other on a dropper loop 18 to 24 inches from the bottom, are very effective when fishing waters frequented by both weakfish and fluke. The flatfish often nail the bottom bait, while the weaks take the high-hook bait.

Grass shrimp constitute a major portion of the diet of weakfish, stripers, and fluke. They're small, and using several on a small hook works very effectively. An option, if you're not able to purchase or obtain grass shrimp locally, is to purchase vacuum-packed frozen shrimp. In the small size they're quite economical and regularly account for many summer flounder and sea trout by anglers who use them.

Tackle and Techniques

Regardless of where you do your bait fishing along the coast, you can maximize your enjoyment by using light tackle in the protected waters of bays and rivers or at the most, medium-weight tackle on open ocean and sound waters. Remember that you're fishing for fun; using heavy, cumbersome tackle would inhibit your enjoyment.

An ideal outfit for fishing big water, where large stripers and blues are your target, is a 6 1/2- to 7-foot-long graphite rod with a medium action, and a multiplying reel loaded with 200 yards of 20-pound-test monofilament.

For bay and river action move down to a popping outfit with a stiff-action graphite rod and small level-wind casting reel. A rod measuring 6 to 6 1/2 feet in overall length and rated for 12- to 15-pound-test line is fine. Any of the many fine level-wind casting reels holding upward of 175 to 200 yards of line is more than adequate. It'll serve you well even with the biggest striper in the ocean. Toward this end, when using light- or medium-weight tackle, maintain a moderate drag setting and don't panic when you hook a big fish. With 200 yards of line it's unlikely that you'll ever get spooled. While the first or second run may consume a lot of line, the fish will eventually stop and you can regain control.

Terminal rigging for using live baits begins with a very simple application. Assuming you're using 15-pound-test line, and in turn want to attach it to a 30-pound-test leader—which is usually double the diameter—it's best to double the end of your line. The best way to accomplish this is to use a loop in the end of your line. A Bimini twist or a surgeon's loop may be used to accomplish this, with the latter being the quicker-to-tie option. This enables you to join the double strand of line to a single strand of leader—with each now having approximately the same diameter. This makes for a stronger connection.

Double the end of your line using a surgeon's loop, and then tie in a 3- or 4-foot-long piece of fluorocarbon leader material, with a surgeon's knot or uni-knot system twice the test of your line. By using a virtually invisible leader of fluorocarbon you can enjoy the luxury of a heavier-test leader, which resists abrasion in the bony jaw of a striper or the tooth-filled mouth of a weakfish. Some anglers use a 6-inch-long piece of No. 8 or 9 coffee-colored stainless-steel wire at the leader's terminal end when targeting bluefish; this prevents them from biting through the fluorocarbon.

The hook of choice for most live baits is a Beak, Live Bait, or Claw style, in sizes ranging from 2/0 through 7/0. With small killies, herring, spot, croaker, and snapper blues, the smaller-sized hooks are appropriate. The larger-sized hooks are perfect when using baits that often weigh 1 to 2 pounds, such as adult menhaden, mackerel, hickory shad, and herring. With all baits, especially eels, tailor the hook size to the bait so it can swim unimpeded.

The easiest method of hooking live bait is running the hook through its lower jaw and out the upper jaw. Some anglers place the hook in the fleshy part of the back, just forward of the dorsal fin, which also works well. These are the two best hooking methods while fishing from a boat, because whether you're drifting or anchored, the baitfish always appears to be swimming naturally. While shore-based anglers often hook a baitfish in the back behind the dorsal fin, if this is done under most boat-fishing conditions it results in the bait being dragged backward. An exception is if you cast the bait toward a jetty and want it to actively swim away from you, toward the rocks where fish may be waiting.

You can also use a treble hook, such as the new Triple Grip Treble, with live baits instead of a single hook. Many feel they have a better hookup ratio with the treble; a single sometimes gets buried into the flesh of the bait as a fish inhales it. With a treble the preferred hooking technique is to place one of the hooks through the head of the bait, forward of the eye. With one of the hooks holding the bait securely, the remaining two hooks are in a position to quickly penetrate as a fish inhales the bait.

Many fish hooked on live bait are deeply hooked. To avoid difficulty in attempting to remove the hook, many anglers leave the barb on only one of the treble's hooks, which is essential to hold the bait on the hook. Use pliers to bend down the barbs on the remaining two hooks. In this way you only have to contend with one barb when removing the hook.

The basic rigging method works nicely when there is minimal current, little drift, and the bait can swim enticingly in an eddy or rip line or over open bottom, lumps, and ridges. When swift currents, a fast drift, or deep water require it, you'll have to add a trolling sinker between the line and leader, which will take the live bait into the depths but won't impair its fish-catching attraction.

Still another method of rigging is to tie a three-way swivel directly to the end of your line, with a short dropper of monofilament tied to a bank- or dipsey-style sinker and the leader tied to the remaining eye. This gets your bait right down on the bottom and proves especially effective in depths ranging from 20 to 60 feet. Match the hook sizes to the targeted species.

Fishing with natural baits from boats presents a challenge. You've got to know the water you plan to fish, take the pains to obtain the best baits, and present them under a wide variety of conditions. Many anglers become so adept at using live, fresh, or frozen bait that they just never use lures, preferring to fool their quarry with the real thing. It's just one of the many exciting challenges that make fishing for the favorite four so much fun.

Delaware River guide Eric Summitt netted this striper for Dick Nelson, who used a live rainbow trout as bait.

III

Fishing
FROM Shore

Al Ristori used a surface darter plug to hook this bluefish while casting on a cool autumn night.

11

CASTING WITH ARTIFICIALS

Walk into any coastal tackle shop and you'll be spellbound by the selection of lures designed to bring strikes from the favorite four. There are literally thousands of lures, many meticulously air-brushed to resemble a particular baitfish. Others have no resemblance to a fish, or anything a fish eats, whatsoever. The hot pink, soft plastic bait tail is a classic example. When attached to the tail of a leadhead jig it's as potent a lure as you'd want to ever use for the favorite four.

A newcomer to saltwater fishing is often perplexed as to what lures to choose and how to fish them. Many initially purchase a wide variety, including plugs, jigs, leadheads, spoons, and plastic baits. Often they're under the mistaken impression that if they have a lot of lures and switch often, they're bound to catch fish. Not so.

Still others become mechanical in their presentation of lures, casting as far as they can, reeling the lure at the same rate of speed, with little regard to water conditions or the action of the lure. Often they're disappointed, too.

Lure Selection

You'll often find that the veteran anglers along the beach can easily be distinguished from the newcomers. The latter come with tackle boxes chock-full of lures, or carry a shoulder bag that causes them to lean much like a mailman, the burden of weight often causing agony. The former often wear but a fly vest, with ample pockets to carry a proven minimal selection that have survived the test of time.

A lure is really little more than metal, plastic, or wood. It's you who has to balance the lure to the outfit you're using to present it, and impart action to the lure to make it resemble something a fish wants to eat. Throughout this chapter a variety of lures that have withstood the test of time will be discussed, along with a basic selection that will serve you well. The techniques that should be used to present this selection of favorites will also be covered. Remember, though, that in the final analysis it's up to you, through trial and error, to determine which lures work best for you. Half the battle is building a confidence level in a basic selection, and knowing that your presentation is on target. After that it's easy.

Mobility is an important part of casting artificials from shore. As such, it's wise to begin with just four or five of each lure type, which makes it manageable to carry them whether you fish from jetties, in the surf, or in bay and river waters. The basic selection should include plugs, metal squids, and leadhead jigs, and may include those with soft plastic, bucktail, or tube tails or skirts, and saltwater flies for use as teasers. The teasers, discussed elsewhere, could well be used in conjunction with almost any lure at any time, whether casting, trolling or jigging, and are guaranteed to enhance your catch.

A fine selection of plugs would include a surface swimmer, subsurface swimmer, darter, popper, mirror, and rattle plug. Armed with these basic types you'll be well served in almost any situation you encounter. This is not to imply that other models aren't effective; the needlefish, flaptail, deep diver, and other models also have their unique applications.

It's important to match the size of the plug to the equipment you're using. These models come in weights ranging from 1/4 to 3/4 ounce for use with a one-handed spinning outfit, on up to 2- and 3-ounce models for fishing the high surf, so be guided accordingly.

The surface swimmer is an exciting plug to fish, and, as the name implies, it works right on the surface. Many plastic plugs carry this name, but by far the best surface swimmers are made of wood and stay on top when retrieved. The key with a surface swimmer is retrieving it at a very slow speed, resulting in a tantalizing side-to-side swimming action, much like an injured baifish struggling on the surface.

While most plugs are carefully air-brushed to resemble a particular baitfish, it has often been said the detailed colors are really designed to catch fishermen. Many veteran anglers will tell you that a bare wooden plug, with the paint chipped and flaked off, often produces extremely well. It's all in the action and the way it's retrieved.

The subsurface swimming plug is available in wood or plastic models. Its lip draws it into the depths, making it a very effective lure when cast or trolled.

Subsurface swimmers are available in shallow-running and deep-running models. The latter have a larger lip and, when retrieved, are drawn into the depths. A slow retrieve is often more effective than a fast one. Don't hesitate to vary the speed. The key is to keep the plug swimming in a lifelike manner, adjusting your retrieve speed to compensate for current and wave action. You can usually feel the plug pulsating as it's retrieved.

The darter is available in both surface and subsurface models. As a result of a V cut in its head, the plug darts from side to side in an irregular manner as it's retrieved, making it irresistible. Vary your speed of retrieve and you'll notice a completely different action.

The popper is a surface plug with a scooped concave head. As it's retrieved, the head pushes water ahead of it. By working your rod tip you can cause the plug to dart ahead, popping water in front of it, and then hesitating at rest until it's popped again. Sometimes a slow, steady retrieve, causing the water to bubble and pop, will bring more strikes than popping it.

The mirror plug model without a lip—your leader is attached to a loop on the top of its head—works in much the same fashion as a leadhead jig. It's made in surface-, medium-, and deep-running models. This plug is especially effective when you want to probe the depths of rivers, inlets, and points of land where a swift rip line occurs. Cast up and across the current, it sinks quickly and will bring strikes as it's swept along, particularly at the end of its swing as it's swept off the bottom.

The rattle plug has much the same design characteristics as the mirror plug, except that several small, metal balls molded into the plug emit a rattling sound as it's retrieved. The plug runs very deep and is especially good when there's heavy surf running or you wish to probe the depths of a river or inlet. It has a shimmering action when slowly retrieved. Or you can whip it, causing it to dart ahead and falter, much like a wounded baitfish, its rattling sound drawing attention.

The greatest majority of plugs are rigged with treble hooks. Depending on the size of the plug, there's usually a treble hook at the rear, with either one or two treble hooks attached to the underside. They're very effective in hooking fish but difficult to remove, especially from a thrashing fish that may have to be released because of size restrictions. Many anglers use pliers to bend down the barbs. This makes removing the hook much easier, yet doesn't impair the hooking or holding quality of the treble hook.

Leadhead jigs come in a wide range of shapes and sizes. Molded with a lead head and a rigged hook, the leadhead's primary purpose is to get deep in the water column, often bouncing the bottom, to draw strikes from the favorite four.

The lead heads of the jigs are molded in a variety of shapes and sizes, ranging from round to lima bean, torpedo, fish head, and others. For the most part it's doubtful that the shape of jig head matters. It does give you the weight to cast and get the lure deep. For purposes of seeking the favorite four your selection should include models ranging from 1/4 to 1 ounce for bay and river applications. For heavy surf and swift current in inlets, models of 2 to 3 ounces are often necessary, with lighter weights being used for most situations.

Leadheads are usually painted all white or yellow, some with a splash of red; others are meticulously painted, and many are just plain lead. The color of the head probably doesn't matter much either. It's the skirt—either bucktail, feathers, soft plastic, or a combination of two or all three—that gives the lure its appeal. Many anglers go a step farther, dressing the hook with a strip of pork rind.

Varying your retrieve is important: Range from slow to fast, with a whip retrieve interspersed. Too often anglers fall into a pattern of just casting and reeling mechanically. It's better to try a slow retrieve, followed by a whip retrieve, followed by a fast retrieve. This presents the lure at different depths in the water column, with three different actions, resulting in more strikes than were you to be constant with your retrieve.

The Charlie Graves block tin squid is but one design of thousands that have for years produced excellent results. Tin squids regularly account for many fine catches for boat anglers and those who cast from shore.

Within the broad category of metal squids is a wide variety of lures. The original metal squids were usually molded of block tin, which has a soft luster and can be brightened when it tarnishes by using a piece of steel wool. The majority of block tin squids are molded with a keel; as they're retrieved, the keel gives them a side-to-side swimming action. Some have a rigid hook molded into the block tin, while other have a free-swinging hook. They're usually dressed with feathers, bucktail, a plastic tube, or a strip of pork rind. The long, thin models are generally referred to as sand eel squids, the short fat ones as butterfish squids, and the medium-sized models as mullet squids, with countless other variations.

Within the framework of this category is a variety of lures, most either hammered stainless-steel jigs or chrome-plated diamond jigs. Their hooks are free swinging, and dressed much the same as the block tin squids. Many come equipped with treble hooks, which for purposes of the species discussed in this book are inappropriate. It's far better to use a single-hook model, because this makes it easier to remove the hook and release undersized or unwanted fish unharmed.

The block tin squids and hammered stainless-steel jigs have an enticing action as they're retrieved. With diamond jigs and slab or Vike jigs there's practically no action, and it's necessary to impart action to the lures using a whip retrieve. Surprisingly, a diamond jig retrieved slowly, with no apparent action, often brings strikes. This is particularly true when sand eels are plentiful in an area. Retrieve the jig slowly so it travels just off the bottom, or right on it, sliding along much like a slithering sand eel.

Lure Presentation

Shore-based anglers are confronted with a wide variety of conditions. They range from presenting a swimming plug on a placid bay with air-clear water to casting a stainless-steel squid into crashing surf fed by a strong onshore wind.

It cannot be stressed too greatly the importance of thinking through each cast you make and methodically planning its retrieve. It's safe to say the majority of shore-based casters are those who fall into a pattern of routinely casting and reeling, seldom paying attention to what they're doing. The repetition of standing in one spot, casting over and over, reeling the same lure through the same water column is usually counterproductive.

Regardless of where you fish from shore—from the surf, jetties, riverbanks, or the shore of a bay—you should plan a strategy. A good way to do this that will pay handsome dividends is to envision an overlay of a piece of graph paper on the water in front of you. Mentally calculate what it will take to present your lure through each block of the graph paper.

By standing in one spot, casting straight out 150 feet, and retrieving your lure, you cover every box directly in front of you that may hold a fish. If you just stand there and repeat yourself and don't catch a fish by the second or third cast, your likelihood of catching a fish on subsequent casts is remote.

Instead, cast at a slight angle to the right of the initial cast and complete your retrieve. Next, do the same to the left of the initial cast, and continue to bracket the area with your casts. This applies on jetties, the surf, the bay—just everywhere you may be fishing. After bracketing in front of you, walk 10 or 20 feet and repeat the procedure. In this way you're almost certain to have the lure working through every possible haunt of a fish feeding or traveling through the waters you're fishing. You cover all the blocks of the graph.

Where a strong tide or current exists, it will carry your lure, and here you've got to incorporate a slightly different approach. A good example is fishing from a jetty on an outgoing tide or at a point of land with the current forming rigs off the point. To cover all the blocks of the graph, you should begin with short casts, beginning by working the lure 20 or 30 feet in front of you, and permitting it to be swept downcurrent as you retrieve. Then extend the cast to 30 or 40 feet, and

Massachusetts enjoys miles of beautiful beaches for surf casting, including Cape Cod and the islands of Cuttyhunk, Martha's Vineyard, and Nantucket.

continue extending until you're reaching out 150 feet or more. This presents your lure in a lifelike pattern, that of a small baitfish either being swept along or struggling to maintain its position in the current.

Very often strikes will come as the plug, leadhead, or metal squid is being slowly worked across the current, and at the end of its swing begins to lift off from the depths and move up in the water column. Stripers, blues, weaks, and fluke stemming the tide and waiting for a meal to be swept their way will be onto the lure in a flash.

When you're fishing heavy surf, or casting to rough water from a jetty, it's important that you maintain control over the lure. Watch the wave action before you cast. As a wave begins to crest, begin your cast; your goal is to position the lure to arch over the wave and drop in behind it. Then promptly take up the slack, maintaining a taut line and total control over the lure's action.

All too often anglers simply cast and retrieve, with their cast going right into the awesome power of a cresting wave. When this happens the lure is pushed toward the beach or jetty, with resulting slack in the line. By the time the slack is reeled up, the incoming waves may well have pushed the lure right onto the beach.

Currents moving along a stretch of beach or jetty often reach speeds of several knots. Here, too, if you just cast out and retrieve, your lures may be swept along in such a manner that they're really not working properly. Instead, cast up into the flow of the current. In this way the current sweeps your lure along as you retrieve, much the same as a forage fish swimming with the current. It also enables you to work your lure deeper, because there's less resistance than you'd experience trying to retrieve against the current, which would usually push the lure to the surface. Imagine that the water in front of you is like a stream, moving from left to right—or right to left, as the case may be—and compensate for this current by casting up into it so that you maintain a taut line and total control of the lure throughout the cast.

When you're casting from a stretch of beach and you approach a jetty, groin, rocky promontory, or dock, remember that this obstruction in the water will divert the normal current from moving along the beach. As a result, there will often be rips and eddies formed where game fish can take up stations, stem the tide, and wait for food to be swept their way.

Sometimes a pocket of quiet water forms on one side of such structures, while just a few feet away the water is churning. It's always important to probe areas such as this, because both bait and your targeted species will often take up stations here.

By all means cast your lure in toward the rocks or groin, right in among the crashing waves, and work the lure back to the beach at an angle. Often the bigger fish will be lying off from such a position, waiting for baitfish to leave what little sanctuary the rocks offer. The same holds true for docks and bridge abutments. Present your lure from both sides of such structures, with the current running toward it, and then away from it. There are dead spots on either side where the bait and forage stem the tide.

By carrying a good selection of lures you're able to probe every level of the water column, from the top to the bottom. You can often begin with a surface-swimming plug, slowly working it through the rips and eddies. Then fish all along the perimeter with a metal squid, and finally probe the fast water and literally bounce the bottom with a leadhead jig. Apply yourself, with slow retrieves where appropriate, speeding up to maintain lure control where necessary and using a whip retrieve intermittently. You just never know what will happen. It may be a 20-pound striper that erupts under the swimmer or a fat fluke that wallops a leadhead bouncing the bottom.

There tends to be a feeling among newcomers to shore fishing that high tide is best because there's more water around jetties, along the beach, or on the flats of coastal bays and rivers. Granted, high tide is a fine time to fish, but so is low tide. Both the top and bottom of the tide present periods of slack water, when just before and after the slack the water is flowing at a more leisurely pace, resulting in fish having to exert less energy to find a meal.

The low-water picture in some places leaves some high-water spots exposed sand. This movement of the water results in the fish continually moving, too. While many areas have what's commonly called thin or shallow water, don't underestimate the potential for this thin water to hold many fish. Huge stripers regularly move inside sandbars paralleling the beach, for they know this is where the baitfish will be. Fluke do the same thing, knowing that the churning surf at low tide will expose sand bugs and crabs, which to them are gourmet treats. When a rattle plug and teaser combo comes slithering across the bottom, they're onto it in a flash.

The longer you fish, the more your confidence will grow. There will be times when just by looking at the water and assessing the stage of the tide and wind direction, you'll know precisely which lure in your arsenal will produce. Many veterans fish for days with the same lure, never changing, for they know that given the bait availability and conditions it's the lure that has produced for them in the past; when the fish are in the mood it'll be the first to produce for them now.

By all means, don't make the mistake of purchasing every lure that comes on the market and is being touted in the media as the lure to end all lures. It doesn't hurt to try, but by expending too much time experimenting and field-testing something new you may be sacrificing good catches with the old-time favorites.

Regardless of which lures you eventually call your favorites, the important thing to remember is making sure those lures cover a lot of bottom, and varying the manner in which they're retrieved. When you're constantly alert and planning a strategy for each cast from shore, you're going to regularly experience that excitement of a game fish walloping your offering.

Casting from the beach while using natural baits is very effective but requires patience.

12

CASTING WITH NATURAL BAITS

Casting from shore, whether a jetty, beach, dock, bridge, or bulkhead, presents many exciting opportunities while using natural baits. While few realize it, the terminal rigging and techniques differ widely from those you'd use fishing natural baits from a boat. From a boat your bait is most often presented either while at anchor or drifting, and your line is generally perpendicular to the bottom, or drifted off at a slight angle. From shore, however, you make a cast and the line is nearly horizontal. In some instances the bait is so large it's virtually impossible to cast. Thus, you need totally different techniques to present big baits to the favorite four from the shore.

Rigs for Baitcasting

There are a number of bottom rigs that are effective, and a basic rig will accommodate a wide variety of baits and situations. The first, and perhaps the most popular, is built around a three-way swivel. Tie a small three-way swivel directly to the end of your line. Next, tie an 8-inch-long piece of light leader material to one eye of the swivel. Tie a surgeon's loop in the terminal end of this short piece, onto which you'll slip your sinker, avoiding the need for a snap.

The sinker style you'll be using will depend on whether you want the rig to be held in place or to be easily retrieved across the bottom.

To dig in and withstand the wave and current pressures, the pyramid-style sinker is ideal. There are several styles of pyramid sinker, all of which are designed to stay in place. For most surf conditions sinkers ranging in weight from 1 to 4 ounces are adequate. There are times, however, when a rough surf requires 5 or 6 ounces or more to hold. Even then, if there's a strong current paralleling the shore or heavy surf caused by an onshore wind, it becomes virtually impossible to hold.

For those occasions when you want to keep your bait moving, you want a sinker that weighs enough to be cast a respectable distance yet slides easily along the bottom when retrieved. The bank-style sinker and the dipsey, which has a small swivel molded into it, are ideal. Here, too, the weights you should include in your surf bag include 1 to 4 ounces for most situations, upping to 5 or 6 ounces when conditions dictate. Anglers fishing with heavy surf tackle sometimes use sinkers heavier than 6 ounces, but these are the exception.

To the remaining eye of the three-way swivel tie in a 36-inch-long piece of fluorocarbon leader material. Tests ranging from 15 to 30 pounds suit most situations, but keep in mind that it's best to use leader material double the test of your line, because it often enters a fish's mouth and can easily be cut by sharp teeth if it's too light. The area fished, species sought, and experience will dictate which test works best for you. Make certain it's fluorocarbon, however, because its refractive index works to your advantage. Fish can't see it, an important consideration, especially when an offshore wind results in calm surf and crystal-clear water conditions.

The final step is to snell a hook of your choice to the end of the leader. Without question the most popular hook styles for a basic surf rig are the Beak or Claw. If you're using a live baitfish, such as a killie, mullet, eel, or spot, it's preferable to use a hook with a plain shank. Should your choice of bait be a sandworm or bloodworm, whole squid, shedder crab, or piece of clam, then select a hook with a baitholder shank. The pair of barbs in the shank holds the bait in place and keeps it from slipping down on the bend of the hook.

The size of the hook should be tailored to the bait you're using. With a live killie, spearing, or sand eel as bait while targeting fluke, a size 1/0 through 3/0 will serve you well. If you're using a whole shedder crab, large clam, or whole squid and hoping for a big striper, it's appropriate to use sizes ranging from 5/0 through 7/0. When blues are in an area but refusing lures, they'll often take a chunk of bunker or herring. Because of the wide range in sizes, you'd best experiment until you determine the size of the fish being taken, and adjust your hook size accordingly.

When you're fishing stationary bait on the bottom, crabs often become a nuisance in that they strip the bait from the hook quickly. To minimize this problem you can add a small Styrofoam or cork float to the leader, placing it approximately 30 inches from the three-way swivel. This will result in the bait being suspended 24 inches off the bottom and hanging down 6 inches, where the movement of the surf and current will cause it to swirl in a lifelike manner. This works particularly well when you're using sandworms, squid, and crabs as bait, because they appear to be swimming naturally. The rig is very effective, however, with any bait you're apt to employ from shore.

One problem with this rig is that as the sinker carries the bait while casting, the bait on occasion will double back on the line and become twisted. You'll waste a lot of effort and time as the bait and rig rest on the bottom in a tangle.

A rig that avoids this problem can be tied with ease. Begin with a 6-foot-long piece of 30-pound-test fluorocarbon leader material. Tie a small black barrel swivel to one end of the leader and a small duolock snap to the other end. Approximately 6 inches from the swivel tie in a large dropper loop that, when completed, will extend 8 or 9 inches from the remaining leader. Move down the leader 20 inches and tie in another dropper loop, the size of which should be the same as the first, extending 8 or 9 inches from the leader. When laid flat, you have the swivel, 6 inches of leader, a dropper loop extending outward 9 inches, followed by 20 inches of leader, another dropper loop extending out 9 inches, and 6 to 8 inches of leader with a duolock snap.

There are two choices to complete the rig. If you want the baits suspended 6 inches off the bottom, simply slip a Styrofoam or cork float onto the dropper loop. If you want the baits to rest on the bottom, then skip the floats.

The final step in preparing the rig is to use either a Claw- or Beak-style hook with a turned-down eye. For striped bass or weakfish a normal shank is fine; if you're targeting bluefish use a long-shank model, which helps keep the fish from biting through the leader.

Slip one hook onto the loop but don't pull it up tight; instead pass the hook through a second time. This results in a bulkiness of the leader material, which, when pulled up tight, holds the hook tightly in place. Were it passed through only once, the hook would have a tendency to slide up instead of being held firmly at the end of the loop. Then repeat the same step on the remaining loop with another hook. Then snap the sinker of your choice onto the duolock snap.

The advantage of this rig is that the sinker is at the end of it; when you make a cast the sinker moves to the target with the leader, dropper loops, and baits trailing, resulting in minimal tangles. Without floats both baits rest on the bottom, and with floats both are suspended. Many anglers fish one of the baits without a float and the other with a float, which gives you the best of both worlds.

While you begin with 6-foot-long piece of leader material, the final rig will measure out around 3 feet in overall length. If tied properly, the hooks on both dropper loops are sufficiently separated that they cannot tangle with each other.

Both of the rigs just described are basically designed to be cast out, permitted to rest on the bottom, retrieved periodically to check the bait and presence of seaweed, and then cast again.

Baitcasting Baits

A wide variety of baits may be used with either of these rigs. The key in bait selection is employing the forage on which the targeted species are feeding at the time you're fishing. For example, early in the season there's limited small-bait activity from menhaden, mullet, sand eels,

The author's wife, June, hooked this nice striper while fishing with a fresh surf clam as bait. Bait fishing takes patience, but the rewards are great.

spot, and other small fish. Striped bass and early-arriving weakfish tend to feed heavily on grass shrimp, sandworms, bloodworms, tapeworms, crabs, clams, and sand bugs. Thus, it behooves you to use the baits on which they're accustomed to feeding, because early-arriving species are scouring the bottom as they search for a meal.

As the season progresses and the favorite four begin to feed on menhaden, herring, mackerel, and other forage species, it's to your advantage to use these species, either as whole baits or as chunks.

Properly baiting your hook is a key consideration in presenting the bait in a natural manner. Sandworms and bloodworms are very delicate but effective baits. It's best to employ a hook with a baitholder shank. These are most often found on Beak- or Claw-style hooks and have two sharp barbs extending from the shank. When you slip the bait onto the hook, these baitholder barbs hold it in place on the shank, not permitting it to slip down into the J part of the hook. With large sandworms, wait until the worm opens its mouth, then slip the hook in, run it down approximately 1 inch, and exit it. The baitholder shank will hold the worm securely, and it will actively swim in the water. If the worms are small, you can add a second one in the same manner.

Because bloodworms are generally smaller than sandworms, the long, thin worms are often impaled on the hook in the middle, with both ends hanging freely; add a second worm if they're small.

Small whole squid are also effective bait. Lightly hook a squid through the head, using a hook with a baitholder shank. Run the hook point into the head and bring it out an inch or two from where it was inserted, depending on the size of the hook and of the squid.

Crabs are also fine bait. Blue and calico crabs are many casters' favorites: They're relatively easy to obtain, either by raking them in the surf, using crab traps, or purchasing them from local bait purveyors. While hard crabs can be used, crabs in the shedder state or (especially) in the soft state—immediately after they molt—are best.

Either a whole crab or piece of crab can be used. After the crab has been placed on the hook it's wise to employ elastic thread to secure it; the force of a cast might otherwise rip the bait from the hook.

Clam meat annually accounts for many of the favorite four. When shucked, the meat of a clam is rather soft, and it tears from the hook easily. To toughen the meat, many anglers use a brine solution of 1 part coarse salt and 1 part tap water. Leave the clams in the heavy brine for a day; the meat becomes tough and remains on the hook. With both fresh clams and brined clams it's wise to use elastic thread to secure the bait to the hook.

Throughout their range, all the species included herein feed extensively on grass shrimp. To use the tiny shrimp as bait requires a very small hook, size 1 or 1/0; thread four or five of the crustaceans onto the hook. Large shrimp, while not native to inshore waters in the Northeast, also make good bait, with a single whole shrimp threaded onto the hook ideal.

There is a divergence of opinion as to whether or not to expose the hook when baiting. Some feel the hook should be buried in the bait and not visible. The more popular approach is to let the point of the hook and barb be exposed, so that the hook is in a position to quickly penetrate as a fish inhales the bait and moves off.

Forage species such as menhaden, mullet, herring, and mackerel—in fact, almost any small fish—can be used as bait for the favorite four. Small, dead baitfish may be used whole. This is the case with sand eels, spearing, rainfish, mummichogs, and other small forage. In the case of larger fish, such as mackerel, herring, and bunker, many anglers find a chunk of bait easier to cast and more effective.

Three sections of forage fish are popularly used as bait: the head, the midsection, and the tail. The midsection chunk is usually the softest and often requires elastic thread to hold it securely to the hook. The tail section also proves effective; with the hook inserted into it, a couple of elastic wraps around tail and hook hold it secure.

The head section, cut at an angle to include the pectoral fin, may be placed on the hook by running it through the lips or eye sockets. Hooked in this way, it stays securely on the hook when cast, without elastic thread. The reason so many anglers favor the head section is not only that it stays on the hook with ease, but also that because of its bony structure, it lasts longer while resting on the bottom in an area frequented by crabs. The crabs can rip and chew on a piece of head bait for a long while, and it's virtually impossible for them to remove it from the hook.

Live forage fish make excellent baits, and the smaller species can be used with some of the rigs just described. This is particularly true with live killies, spots, and croaker. But as you move into large forage, such as eels, adult menhaden, mackerel, and herring—which can weigh over a pound—it becomes virtually impossible to effectively cast. There are exceptions, however, in that many jetty casters, dock anglers, and pier anglers will live-line the bait. This is a delicate procedure; if you pressure a cast to achieve distance, you invariably rip the bait from the hook.

Those who prefer live-lining most often employ a 36- to 48-inch-long 30-pound-test fluorocarbon leader. Tie this to the line by first using a surgeon's loop to double the last foot or two of your terminal line, and then using a surgeon's knot to join line and leader.

The hook, most often a Claw, Beak, O'Shaughnessy, or Circle style, is tied to the end of the leader using a uni-knot. You can also employ a treble hook with live bait: Use one of the three hooks to impale the bait, with the remaining two hooks in position to penetrate once a fish inhales the bait.

The conditions will often determine just how you should hook the live bait for live-lining purposes. In a river with a swift current, it's advantageous to hook the baitfish so that it can swim effectively and appears to be stemming the tide or current. This is best accomplished by running the hook through the lower jaw and out the upper, through the eye sockets, or through the skin above the eyes.

If, however, you're casting from a pier or jetty, where there's minimal current, and you wish the baitfish to swim away from the structure, then it's appropriate to place the hook in the back of the baitfish between the dorsal fin and tail. This enables the baitfish to swim away from the structure unimpeded, and requires minimal casting.

Using this technique, a caster will often pull back gently as the baitfish attempts to swim away, which encourages the baitfish to become more aggressive and swim away from the structure—exactly what you want it to do. This approach works particularly well with live menhaden, hickory shad, herring, mackerel, and eels.

You'll find that live bait will often settle into a pattern of leisurely swimming about, unconcerned that it is, in fact, on a hook. When approached by a predator, a big striper or blue, the bunker, mackerel, hickory shad, or other baitfish will excitedly swim about at an accelerated rate of speed, often breaking the water as it attempts to elude.

This is when you must be patient. While bluefish will often charge the bait, big stripers will often toy with it, watching it and circling before ultimately making a decision to engulf it. You've got to keep your reel in free spool and let the bait swim freely, unimpeded. Once the fish has taken the bait and moved off, it's wise to hesitate, and hesitate some more, for at least a 10-count. Then point the rod in the direction the line is moving, lock the reel into gear, and lift back smartly to set the hook. If you've timed it correctly, the rod will be practically ripped from your hands as the lunker moves off.

Breeches Buoy Rig

A rather unique technique for presenting the big live bait from shore, pier, or jetty is to use what's popularly referred to as a breeches buoy rig. The rig uses the same principle as a breeches buoy, moving an object from one place to another on a line, using the angle of descent, coupled with the weight of the object, as the propellant.

To prepare a breeches buoy rig, begin by tying a duolock snap directly onto the end of your line using a uni-knot. For this type of fishing, 30-pound-test line is preferred because there's some additional friction and pressure on the line. Then snap on a pyramid-style sinker.

To make up the leader, begin with a piece of 30-pound-test fluorocarbon. Tie a combination barrel swivel and coastlock snap to one end of the leader and your hook of choice to the other.

Bait up the hook as discussed earlier. The method of choice for this type of rig is to place the hook in the fleshy part of the back either before or behind the dorsal fin, enabling the fish to swim about unimpeded.

The next step may sound unusual. Determine where you want the bait to be, and cast your sinker to that spot, without any rig attached whatsoever. The final step is to open the coastlock snap attached to the leader, place it around the line between the tip of your rod and the sinker—which may be 100 feet or more away—and snap the coastlock snap shut. Lift the rod tip into the air and pull the line taut while releasing the fish attached to

The breeches buoy rig is effective for delivering your live bait far from shore, without injury to the bait. A sinker is tied to the end of your line and cast out. Then the coastlock snap is attached to the line, and the entire rig and live bait slides down the line and swims off, until a hungry striper or blue finds it.

the breeches buoy leader rig. It will gently slide down into the water.

As soon as it enters the water, the baitfish will begin swimming about vigorously. It can swim all the way to the end of the line where it meets the sinker, or it can simply swim back and forth along the length of line that's in the water. Sometimes it will excitedly swim about where the line enters the water, making a surface commotion that often attracts predators to it.

When it's not in view, you can tell that it's still there by maintaining a taut line, feeling the vibrations as the baitfish moves about. Sometimes it's wise to provide some slack: Let the line settle horizontally to the bottom, with the baitfish moving back and forth along the bottom. Then pull the line taut again; the baitfish will feel the pressure and excitedly begin to move about.

As one of the big four picks up the baitfish and moves off with it, there's a possibility you may hardly feel the movement, particularly if it moves in the direction your line is pointed. Once it gets to the end and the coastlock snap comes up tight against the duolock snap and sinker, you'll get a jolt that often startles you, especially if you haven't had a strike for hours. Toward this end it's wise to keep the reel locked into gear with a moderate drag setting, for when it comes taut the fish has usually already taken the bait well into its mouth. Quite often it has already hooked itself.

This method is extremely effective, even with small baitfish. Often during the fall of the year, when huge schools of rainfish, mullet, and menhaden are moving along the beach, it's possible to snag them using a weighted treble hook or the treble hooks of a plug that you yank through a tightly packed school.

The effective technique is to snag a 5- or 6-inch-long baitfish, place it on the breeches buoy rig, and position it just beyond the spot where the school of baitfish is herded tight to the beach. Here the struggling baitfish, off by itself away from the school, often results in an immediate strike, because stripers, blues, or weaks often regroup off and away from the main school they're stalking. They find an unsuspecting single fish an easy target.

Rigs for Fluke

Fluke are regularly taken on natural baits cast from shore. Surprisingly, while most anglers realize boatmen who drift and in turn cover a lot of water enjoy great success, many casters make the mistake of casting their fluke bait from the surf, jetty, pier, or bridge and leaving it motionless. This greatly reduces their chance at scoring. It's far better to present the natural bait on the bottom, constantly casting and retrieving it so that it covers a lot of bottom. You want to put it in front of a flatfish searching for a meal.

One of the most popular rigs is affectionately called the Sneaky Pete. Popularized by Ernie Wuesthof, the sage of the Tackle Shop in Normandy Beach, New Jersey, it is without question one of the most successful casting rigs you can use for fluke while fishing from shore.

The rig consists of a tiny three-way swivel with a connecting link on one eye of the swivel to which is attached a small dipsey-style sinker, just heavy enough to enable you to cast a reasonable distance. To the remaining eye of the swivel tie a 30-inch-long piece of 30-pound fluorocarbon leader material. A small bead is slipped onto the leader, followed by a thumbnail-sized chartreuse Colorado spinner blade, followed by

The Sneaky Pete fluke rig derives its name from having a pair of hooks rigged in tandem. The spinner blade is the attractor: as a fluke strikes the strip bait, it's invariably hooked on the tail hook.

four additional beads. The rig is completed by snelling a size 1, 1/0, or 2/0 Claw-style hook to the leader, followed by a second hook 2 inches behind the first.

Favored bait for this rig consists of a strip of freshly caught sea robin, dogfish, herring, or squid. The bait should never be more than 1/2 inch wide, so that the hook cannot be buried into the bait as it lies over. The strip should be cut in a torpedo shape, approximately 4 inches in length. Impale the first hook—nearest the Colorado spinner—into the head of the strip bait, and the second (the trailing hook) into the midsection of the strip bait so the entire strip lies flat. As you can appreciate, the name Sneaky Pete evolved because the trailing hook is sneaky; it's invariably the one that hooks the fluke as it takes the fluttering bait. Using the same rig with the bait on but a single hook results in many missed strikes, because the fluke strikes the trailing section of strip.

You've got to work this bait rig much like an artificial. There're two effective retrieving techniques, and it pays to alternate between them. First, cast out and simply reel the rig back in a slow and deliberate retrieve. The other approach is a whip retrieve. Cast out, let the rig settle to the bottom, then smartly move your tip forward 5 or 6 feet, take up the slack, and repeat the procedure.

When casting from the surf in particularly, you'll often find that the fluke are feeding right along the edge of the drop-off just a few feet from where you're standing: The churning action of the waves is constantly exposing the crabs, sand bugs, and grass shrimp on which summer flounder feed. Small forage species such as sand eels, spearing, mullet, and rainfish also hold tight to the edge of the beach to avoid the predators traveling along the surf line.

It becomes important that you work the rig right to the beach. With a jigging retrieve, the fluke will give you a jolt as it strikes. When you're using a slow, steady retrieve, the strike as the fluke mouths the bait will often feel like you've snagged bottom. Here it's important to resist the urge to strike the fish; just continue reeling. As the fish feels the bait continuing to move, it reacts much the way it would if a small forage fish were attempting to get away: It strikes all the harder, and becomes hooked in the bargain.

Using natural baits from shore and employing the rigs just discussed is challenging, but must be combined with knowing the structure and water you plan to fish. Whether it be a stretch of surf, jetty, or groin, the local gas dock or a busy bridge, the more you study the water and know the bottom conformation, the more successful you'll be with natural baits. Recognizing that the rough surf provides a great opportunity for scoring with clams enables you to score while anglers using lures often fail. Likewise, using a breeches buoy to carry big live bait far from where you're standing puts you at a great advantage. It's all part of a learning process that never ceases, which makes fishing with natural baits from shore so much of a challenge . . . and so much fun.

First light is perhaps the best time of day to be fishing for the big four from coastal jetties, as the fish are usually most active at that time.

13

FISHING A JETTY OR GROIN

Of the many techniques employed to catch the Northeast's favorite four, fishing from jetties and groins is without a doubt the most challenging and exciting. These man-made structures, built of rock, wood and pilings, or concrete, extend seaward along the ocean to hold back its ravaging effects on the land. Jetties are designed to prevent inlets from shoaling, and groins to prevent beach erosion. Nature also provides rocky promontories that extend seaward, from which many anglers fish. Then, too, there are breakwaters in many bays, designed to prevent tidal surges from entering harbors. All provide a platform from which to cast.

All of these structures ultimately become habitat for a variety of marine growth, such as sea moss, barnacles, and mussels. Scattered

There are thousands of jetties and groins along the coast, and you can be certain there's a population of the favorite four close at hand. A selection of tackle prepares you for all conditions.

among the submerged rocks, crabs and lobsters seek shelter in the crevices. Tautog, cunner, and sheepshead also take up residence among the rocks, and are often sought as food by our targeted species. Many forage species, such as sand eels, spearing, menhaden, rainfish, and other small fish, often swim in tightly packed schools up close to the rocks to avoid the onslaughts of the predatory species.

Before I get into the specifics of terminal rigging, it's appropriate to discuss why fish linger around jetties and groins. Most often it's because food is readily available, given the variety of forage species that make the waters around the rocks their home. At other times schools of forage species—such as mullet, menhaden, rainfish, and spearing—traveling up and down the beach must of necessity travel around the fronts of rock piles. Stripers, blues, and weakfish know this, and they'll often take up stations along the seaward corners of jetties, waiting to intercept the traveling schools of bait.

This is where the jetty caster's technique differs from that of the surf angler. The latter may have to cast a long distance, sometimes across an outer bar. For the jetty fisherman, concentrating cast and presentation in that magic area from the jetty rocks out perhaps 150 feet is critical. This is the range most often frequented by hungry game fish. Indeed, many strikes from all three species will come as your lure or bait approaches to within 25 feet of where you're standing.

Jetties such as this, at the entrance to Montauk's harbor, are located at hundreds of inlets along the coast. They make fine casting platforms that produce great catches.

Many newcomers to jetty fishing try to cast as far as possible, to keep their lure or bait away from the rocks; during the retrieve they speed up to avoid the possibility of becoming fouled in the rocks. This approach is to be discouraged, because often the game fish are moving close to the rocks. This is especially the case around older jetties, where many of the rocks have been tumbled about the structure's perimeter. You're far better served by making many relatively short casts and working the lure right to the edge of the rocks. In this way you're making twice the number of casts and almost always have the lure in the strike range.

There's nothing wrong with occasionally leaning into a cast and reaching far out, but this should be minimal—unless, of course, you find that a particular jetty consistently pays off for the long cast, such as where a natural rocky bottom exists a couple of hundred feet from the jetty. Stripers and weakfish will often take up residence among the rocks, with summer flounder along the perimeter.

Moving on Jetties

The anglers who cast from jetties are affectionately known as "jetty jockeys." They climb from rock to rock, occasionally on all fours as they traverse a deep crevice. Mobility is the key, and tackle boxes or buckets are simply not practical. Most rock climbers carry their gear in a shoulder bag or a multipocketed fishing vest, every pocket filled with hooks, leaders, lures, pliers, and other essentials.

Perhaps the most important piece of equipment for jetty fishermen is footwear. The rocks located between the high-water and low-water tide lines are often covered with moss and mussels, with the former being very slippery. To better secure their footing, anglers often wear strap-on ice creepers over their boots or shoes. Many simply wear an economical pair of golf shoes, the aluminum cleats securing their feet as they climb from rock to rock. Some anglers go so far as to have the local shoemaker cement a pair of golf soles to the soles of their boots. The golf cleats eventually wear down, and are easily replaced using a wrench that removes the worn cleat from the sole and tightens on a new one.

While coastal jetties make extraordinary fishing platforms, a great deal of care should be taken when traversing them. Cleated footwear is an excellent beginning, and when the weather is inclement, with the strong surf and wind-tossed waves buffeting the rocks, a storm suit is a must. Still another precautionary measure is to pay heed to the stage of the tide. The seaward ends of many groins are higher than the rocks along the beach. While access is easy at low tide, the flooding tide often rises 3 or 4 feet along the beach, making it virtually impossible to get off the jetty as the tide floods. Also pay heed to onshore winds and heavy surf. During a flooding tide, green water may cascade over a low jetty, with the potential of washing a person from the rocks.

Tackle and Technique

The ideal casting outfit for jetty fishing centers on a rod in the 7- to 8-foot range, with either a conventional or a spinning reel capable of holding 250 yards of 15-, 17-, or 20-pound-test line. A medium-action rod, preferably of graphite, that can cast anything from 1/2-ounce on up to 3-ounces is ideal and will handle both bait fishing and lure applications.

This is not to say that a light one-handed casting rod can't be used from a bay breakwater, or that a 9-footer isn't better suited to a high-off-the-water inlet rock pile with many tumbled boulders in front of you. Tailor the tackle to the situation you encounter.

The tendency to use lines testing 15-pounds or heavier comes about because on occasion the line will be dragged across rocks, moss and mussels as you retrieve. Occasionally your lure will snag on a mussel, and with light lines it often means a lost lure or rig. With heavier line you're often able to pull the lure free.

Many jetty fishermen employ 3- or 4-feet of double line before tying on their terminal tackle. A double surgeons knot is ideal for tying the double line, as it is easy to tie and maintains excellent knot strength. A Uni-Knot is then used to tie the double line to the swivel of your leader or bottom rig.

Once you're equipped it's wise to visit the jetties you plan to fish when the tide is low, so you can make a visual note of spots to avoid. Some groins and jetties may not have suffered the ravages of the ocean, and at low tide are neat, with each rock in place. The majority, however, will have some of the rocks tossed about like pebbles. By making a visual reference you'll know where rocks are submerged and invisible at high tide. Then you can avoid casts that may immediately become snagged in an area through which it's virtually impossible to retrieve a lure. This knowledge is also helpful, when you're fighting a big striper or blue: You can lead the fish away from spots where the mussel- and barnacle-covered rocks might sever your line.

Each jetty has a personality of its own. Many have a sandy shoal on one side, and a deep cut with a swift current on the other. By observing the differences at low tide you can plan a casting strategy—an especially important consideration when you'll be casting into the dark waters of night tides.

Coaxing game fish to strike lures while casting from coastal jetties is a challenge so exciting that many anglers forgo all other techniques.

The most popular lures at the disposal of the jetty fraternity include metal squids, plugs, and leadhead jigs. Within these three lure categories are dozens of combinations. As a case in point, metal squids include the time-proven molded block tin squids, hammered stainless-steel jigs, chrome- and gold-plated jigs, and assorted variations on the diamond jig. Some of these lures are fished plain, others by adding to the hook a plastic bait tail, a plastic tube tail, feathers, a bucktail skirt, or a piece of pork rind. The lures are available in sizes ranging from 1/4 ounce to 3 or 4 ounces. Here it becomes a matter of choosing the lure that most closely resembles the baitfish in residence in size and color.

Dozens of plug models also coax strikes from the favorite species. Perhaps the most popular plug in use today is the swimming plug, which when retrieved has a side-to-side swimming action brought into play by its lip. These plugs are available in surface-swimming, intermediate, and deep-diving models, some solid, others jointed. They come in every color of the rainbow, either to replicate natural baitfish or simply to excite a feeding frenzy through their gaudiness, with no resemblance to a baitfish whatsoever. Sizes range from a mere inch in length to imitate tiny fry on up to 7- or 8-inch models that resemble menhaden, herring, mackerel, and mullet.

Then, too, there are popping plugs, darters, flaptail plugs, bullet plugs, mirror plugs, pencil plugs, and a host of other variations. All are fun to use, and each requires a different retrieve technique to maximize its action and draw strikes. Here it's important to note that mastering the technique of retrieving a lure is critical. It's not just a matter of casting out and reeling in, which is a trap many anglers fall into. Each lure works differently, some requiring an extremely slow retrieve, others a fast one, while some work best when worked with an irregular retrieve, causing the plug to swim ahead then falter, much like an injured or distressed baitfish.

Just as the block tin squid has evolved over time, so has the leadhead jig. For years the bucktail jig was the standard—a lead head with a bucktail skirt. With the advent of plastics and the plastic bait tail, the bucktail jig lost favor and the leadhead jig became the standard.

The basic leadhead jig, as its name implies, is a lead head molded around a hook, with either a bucktail, a soft plastic tail, or a pork rind skirt. They're made in a wide variety of shapes. Some are left unpainted, while others are painted solid colors, with white and yellow the most popular. Still others are air-brushed to replicate a variety of baitfish, right down to the mouth and eyes.

Over time plastic bait tails have replaced the bucktail and feathers used on many jigs, as the latter are more time consuming to produce. With the plastic tails you just select the size and finish you wish, slip the tail onto the hook of the leadhead, and you're ready to go. The plastic tails are made to exactly replicate many baitfish such as sand eels, herring, mullet, and others. Some tails are made in multicolored shades, some with sparkles, to resemble almost any fry.

Jetty fishermen and surf fishermen regularly employ lures in combination. With a plug or metal squid as the primary lure, a plastic bait tail, strip of pork rind, or saltwater fly is employed as a teaser 24 to 30 inches ahead.

You'll need two small black duolock snaps, a tiny black barrel swivel, and 48 inches of fluorocarbon leader material to make up the leader. While you may waste a bit of leader, it's much easier to tie knots if you begin with more than you need.

Begin by slipping the swivel onto the leader and positioning it approximately 12 inches from the end. Next, tie a dropper loop by making a loop with the swivel inside it, using four turns of leader, bringing the swivel through the center, and having it extend 1/4 inch from the tightened knot. When complete you should have the swivel on the dropper loop, with a short length of leader for the dropper, and a long length of leader for the primary lure.

Complete the leader by using a uni-knot to tie a small duolock snap to the shorter end of the leader onto which the teaser will be attached. Next, tie a somewhat larger duolock snap to the longer part of the leader onto which the primary lure will be attached.

The teaser may be a saltwater fly such as a Clouser, Deceiver, or streamer; a plastic bait tail; or even just a strip of pork rind on a hook.

The rigged eel is popular with jetty fishermen and can also be trolled with good results. Many anglers rig fresh eels and keep them in a kosher salt brine solution. Soft plastic eels rigged in the same manner are also effective.

Teasers tied or rigged on size 1/0 through 3/0 O'Shaughnessy hooks are favored. With this combination the teaser sometimes gets the strikes, and sometimes it's the primary lure. It's not unusual to hook a "double-header"—a fish on each lure.

While live eels are used effectively for striped bass and weakfish, around rock piles many anglers employ dead rigged eels with great results. The common eels ranging in length from 6 to 18 inches are killed in salt brine. They are then rigged on metal squids designed expressly for this purpose. Place a metal squid's hook in the head of the eel and run a second hook through the eel with a rigging needle so that it comes out near the eel's vent. Rigged in this manner the rigged eel is a combination lure and bait. Cast and retrieve it much as you would a plug or metal squid; it's very effective along many areas of the coast.

Anglers generally keep six to a dozen eels rigged and stored in kosher salt brine in 1-gallon plastic mayonnaise jars. These jars are easily obtained at almost any delicatessen. Rigged and stored in this manner, the eels are tough and keep for months at a time.

No two jetties are alike, and it takes a while to master the techniques of fishing each. Keep in mind that fish are attracted to a jetty because forage species often seek the protection of the rocks; crabs, lobsters, sand fleas, and shrimp are also readily available.

There's no way of knowing precisely where the fish will be feeding. This makes it very important that you thoroughly cover all the water surrounding the jetty. Make your first cast shortly after you walk out onto the jetty, placing your lure just outside the curl of the breakers working in toward the beach. Often the churning action of the waves exposes sand fleas, crabs, and shrimp, and fish will move right into the heavy water to feed.

After several casts, move out onto the jetty and bracket your casts, first casting in toward the beach so the retrieve almost parallels the jetty. Next place a cast at a 45-degree angle to the left of where you're standing, then straight in front of you, and to the right 45 degrees, and finally almost paralleling the jetty. Then move out and repeat the procedure. As you approach the end of the jetty, you'll often find a situation in which the seas are crashing onto the rocks and it's difficult to cast over the submerged rocks and work your lure. But this is a spot that you should work carefully, because big striped bass and weakfish often feed among the tumbled rocks of the jetty front. Complete the circuit and work the remaining side of the jetty to the beach.

Over time you'll find that you receive strikes at different spots on each jetty. Sometimes it's the location of submerged rocks and the way currents swirl around them that results in fish taking up feeding stations. As you accumulate information about each jetty, you can concentrate your efforts on the spots and lures that regularly produce strikes.

It's important to make each cast count. A fish feeding in a pocket adjacent to a jetty will often strike on your first cast. Veteran jetty jockeys will tell you that the first cast to any area often results in a strike: A fish is actively searching for a meal, and as your lure comes into range it's onto it in a flash. Working your lure properly means working it right to the very edge of the rocks before lifting it from the water.

Newcomers often make the mistake of reeling quickly as their lure approaches the rocks, to avoid getting fouled. This is a big mistake, because by far the greatest number of strikes come close in. Sometimes the fish are feeding close in, but more often a game fish is attracted to and follows the lure. When the fish realizes that the lure appears to be seeking the sanctuary of the rocks, it makes a last-second lunge to prevent the meal from getting away. Huge stripers often startle you as they crash a lure within a rod's length of where you're standing, an exciting experience that really gets the adrenaline moving.

It's always wise to carry a 6-foot-long piece of plastic-covered clothesline with you. This makes an excellent stringer for the fish you want to retain for the dinner table.

Many anglers who target large fish also carry a long-handled gaff. A 6- to 8-foot-long handle of lightweight bamboo with a 2- or 3-inch stainless-steel gaff hook is ideal. A gaff of this size gives you the reach to land a big fish that you've led to the rocks, especially when heavy surf is running. Take care never to use a gaff unless you're absolutely certain the fish exceeds the minimum size restrictions of the state in which you're fishing.

Techniques for Inlet Jetties

Surf fishermen and jetty jockeys are often shut out of their favorite haunts when a rip-roaring nor'easter or tropical storm churns their water to froth. It's then that many of them turn to coastal inlet jetties, because these inlets are usually fishable, especially on the ebbing tide.

Several things happen on the ebb. The often roiled, dirty water that enters the river on the flood has a chance to settle; on the ebb it's usually cleaner. Also, an ebb current carries a mass of forage seaward. Sometimes you can stand on a bridge, dock, or bulkhead near the spot where the river flows through the inlet to the ocean and observe what's happening. The current carries crabs, thousands of tiny grass shrimp, and seaworms beyond count straight toward the stripers, weaks, fluke, and bluefish schooled up in the inlet waiting for a meal.

You can also observe thousands upon thousands of spearing and rainfish packed tight against the jetty rocks, often turning a quiet night noisy as they flutter excitedly on the surface. The baitfish are well aware that if they venture from the sanctuary the rocks offer, they're doomed.

Perhaps 90 percent or more of the anglers fishing the inlets on the dropping tide minimize their chances of scoring by employing normal surf and jetty techniques, which just don't work well in the inlets. They're casting tiny surface-swimming plugs, 1/2-ounce jigs, rigged eels, metal squids, and a host of other lures that are usually working far above—sometimes 15 or 20 feet above—where the fish are actually feeding. In this game you've got to get down to the bottom, which is where the fish are holding and waiting for food to be swept their way. The leadhead jig is the lure of choice, especially when the tide is running swiftly. This jig plummets to the bottom quickly and is easily worked through the depths at which the fish are feeding.

While the lure is important, so is the presentation. Many anglers make the mistake of getting onto an inlet's rock piles and fishing as though they were programmed. Cast and retrieve, cast and retrieve, over and over. The lure covers the same water again and again, often never coming in range of fish that may be feeding just a few feet from where they're standing.

Seldom should you make more than three or four casts of the same distance when fishing an ebbing tide in the inlets. Instead, employ the same technique popularized by trout fishermen with a free-drifting nymph. First, make a short cast across and somewhat downcurrent, permitting the lure to sink and the current to carry it along until it lifts off the bottom at the end of the swing. On the next cast extend the distance 5 feet or so, letting the lure cover new water. Repeat this process until you're extending the cast as far as you can with a leadhead jig.

Then it's a matter of moving 10 feet or more out on the jetty or back up the river, as the case may be, and repeating the same process. Over time this gets your leadhead jig over practically every piece of inlet bottom where bass, blues, fluke, or weaks may be holding. Invariably the strike comes at the end of the swing, as the jig lifts off the bottom. Often it feels like you're snagged; as you lift back, though, you feel a jarring jolt and you're in solidly, not to the bottom but to a bucking adversary!

Instead of a leader, many inlet casters employ a shot of 20-pound-test monofilament that's about 1 1/2 times the length of their rod. This is secured with a double surgeon's knot to the 15- or 17-pound-test monofilament spooled on the reel. This shock line takes the abuse when you're casting or dragging across mussel-covered rocks. It also allows you to lift 3- to 6-pound fish with ease, enabling a quick release. Use a small duolock stainless-steel snap at the end of the shock leader to facilitate changing lures at different stages of the tide.

Patience is the key in inlets. Many make the mistake of arriving at the top of the tide, assuming that fish will immediately take up stations and begin feeding on the ebb. Not so. Occasionally the fish will be there, but more often than not they'll take up stations as the tide begins to fall. Remember that in heavy water—swiftly flowing current—a fish has to expend a tremendous amount of energy to hold its position. Thus, they'll wait and take up stations when the current begins to ease.

The last couple of hours of the ebb often produce the most hectic action. By this time the water has fallen to the point that you can climb down low on the rocks, with secure footing on the mussel-covered rocks that are exposed. Toward this end, make absolutely certain that you always wear jetty creepers—those with golf soles are perfect—when working the rock piles. It's just unsafe climbing around slippery rocks in the dark of night in sneakers.

At this stage of the tide the current is gliding nicely seaward, lots of bait has moved with it, and more often than not the fish are in position. When you arrive, especially on a late tide, you may have the entire inlet to yourself. Often you'll be into a fish on your very first cast. Then it can be nonstop action for a couple of hours, with a mixed bag of the favorite four.

In inlet fishing there are many variables, and no two tides are alike. During a full moon the tide is sometimes so fast that it looks like the entire river is emptying out. On such occasions you may have to use a heavier leadhead jig, one weighing 2 or 3 ounces, to get it down deep and bouncing the bottom as the current carries it seaward. Remember that if you don't feel it hitting the bottom, then lifting off, drifting a bit, and bouncing again, it's not in the strike zone; a heavier jig may be needed. Keep the line taut and reel slowly, so you've got good control. As the current slows or on nights when there's little current, you may find that a 1/2- or 1-ounce leadhead performs better, so make adjustments accordingly.

As the tide approaches slack, try a deep-swimming plug or metal squid and pork rind. The key is casting out and letting the lure settle into the depths before you begin the retrieve. Most often this is effective on either side of the slack-water period, high or low.

Not to be forgotten are the pockets on the ocean side of inlets. Sometimes the fish move from the inlet to feed on baitfish that seek shelter among the rocks and tight to the beach on both sides of the jetties. If working a conventional bouncing leadhead on an outgoing tide isn't giving you results, don't hesitate to walk to the other side of the jetty and give that a whirl. When the inlet proper isn't producing, it often pays to walk down to the beach and either plug or squid it for a couple of hundred feet. Sometimes you'll be surprised with the rewards when surf conditions permit.

No matter where you find a jetty, groin, rocky promontory, or break-water along the coast, you're sure to find the favorite four—or at least a couple of them—in residence. Master the techniques and you'll open a new horizon in what is unquestionably the most challenging and exciting of coastal angling experiences.

There are more than a thousand miles of surf that striped bass, bluefish, weakfish and fluke call home, with plenty of room for everyone.

14

FISHING A STRETCH OF SURF

Reaching from the Carolinas on north to Maine are more than a thousand miles of beautiful beaches. They beckon anglers who like to trudge over the dunes and walk the beach, casting to the crashing surf for their favorite four. While striped bass, bluefish, weakfish, and summer flounder frequent bay and river waters along with the open ocean, they are equally at home in the ever-changing surf, where they find an abundance of forage to satisfy their appetites.

Scouting the Beach

All these miles of beaches offer a surf fisherman the opportunity to find peace and solitude as he seeks his favorite. Many surfing hot spots are easily accessible, and they draw great crowds. Indeed, it's not uncommon at many spots to observe anglers standing shoulder to shoulder as they cast to the breakers.

But there are also hundreds upon hundreds of miles of desolate beach where you'll seldom encounter other anglers. You may have to walk 1/4 mile or so to reach them, or perhaps they're only accessible via beach buggy. What they offer is the ultimate in surf fishing, where it's just you, the beach, and the challenge of utilizing your skills to read the water and determine where to concentrate your efforts.

The key to maximizing your enjoyment of the surf is taking the time to scout an area you plan to fish. If you develop an intimate knowledge of the water, you can work a productive stretch of beach and score whether you fish day or night, high tide or low tide, rough surf or calm. This is easier than it sounds—all you have to do is invest a couple of hours learning the lay of the beach.

Select a bright, sunny day to do your survey work, and be on the beach at dead low tide. You'll be pleasantly surprised how much you can learn just by looking. Make it a point to work 1 1/2 to 2 miles of beach. In a stretch of this length you'll find some spots that drop off abruptly—spots where from the high-water to the low-water mark is an almost clifflike drop-off, and then a gentle slope into the sea. Other spots will just gradually slope into the ocean.

Many sections of coast have bar formations paralleling the beach. No two bar formations are alike, but most have some common characteristics. When observed at low tide the sandbars are occasionally exposed and the surf crashes in on them, rolling across and dumping tons of water inside them, into sluices. This water is trapped inside the bar with nowhere to go, unless the bar has breaks, often called holes or cuts. Thus, as a wave crashes across the bar, the water fol-

A wave can be seen breaking on the sandbar as Ralph Robinson unhooks a nice fluke he landed on a Sneaky Pete rig inside the bar, no more than 25 feet from the beach.

lows the path of least resistance and moves toward the break. This action often causes what are popularly called rip tides along the beach, which regularly present problems to any swimmers unexpectedly caught in the extremely swift current.

Picture for a moment two sandbars several hundred feet long, extending parallel to the beach and approximately 100 feet away from it at low tide. At some point the center of each bar formation will extend toward the beach, where the water is only a foot or two deep. However, as the bar continues parallel with the beach, there's often a break in it. This is usually 50 to 75 feet wide and quite deep—5 to 15 feet at low tide. Each break in the bar varies in size and depth, but represents the path the fish will follow to access the forage-filled waters inside the bar.

As the waves crash across both bars, the water crashing across the bar to your left will flow to the right toward the break, while the water crashing across the bar to your right will flow left toward the same break and exit seaward. You'll readily notice this as you cast and retrieve, for your lure will be carried along with the current formed as the water rushes to exit through the break. When you observe this at low tide you can begin to understand what's happening, because it's clearly visible, which isn't the case at high tide. However, the same current forms even during high tide. The onrushing water continues to move and exit through the breaks.

While along the majority of the coast you'll find but a single bar formation paralleling the beach, the distance of bars from shore varies. There are coastal areas, especially at spots such as Hatteras, North Carolina, where series of bar formations extend seaward for a mile or more. The favorite four you're seeking find all bar formations to their liking, for the constant crashing action of the waves regularly exposes forage such as clams, crabs, shrimp, seaworms, and sand bugs. In addition, forage species like mullet, spearing, menhaden, sand eels, and rainfish seek what little protection they can find along the beach, often schooling inside a bar or swimming in tightly knit schools in the shallows along the edge of the drop-off just a few feet from the sand.

All the favored species move extensively as they feed on various stages of the tide. At extremely low tide there may not be sufficient water inside the bars for them to feed, so they'll work along the outer edge of a bar or in the deep holes and cuts between bars. As the tide floods, the fish will move through the breaks and work up and down the sluices to feed on the abundance of forage that seeks the sanctuary of the shallows.

By thoroughly understanding beach formations, you'll know just where to apply your efforts at various stages of the tide and under different surf conditions. By all means take the time to scout the areas of surf you plan to fish. A couple of hours at low tide will pay handsome dividends. Also keep in mind that the surf formations are constantly changing. A deep cut, sluice, or drop-off that may have produced fantastic sport for weeks on end may completely disappear as a result of a heavy storm. Nor'easters with winds in excess of 35 miles per hour and tropical storms will erode and reconfigure beaches, and you'll have to begin all over again. This is all part of surf fishing. The angler who recognizes that conditions always change, and adapts his techniques accordingly, will be far more successful than the casual angler who adapts an attitude that it doesn't matter.

Surf Tackle and Techniques

Surf fishermen generally employ one of three basic outfits while casting from the beach: heavy, medium, or light. Several factors enter into determining just which outfit to use, including surf conditions, the size of the species sought, and the lures being used.

Heavy surf rods range in length from 9 to 13 feet. They're built for two-handed casting, with butt sections measuring from 24 to 36 inches in length, depending on the rod's action and whether it was designed for a spinning or multiplying reel.

The tip sections of heavy surf rods are stiff and powerful, for they're called upon to deliver a range of weights from 1 to upward of 8 ounces. With such a great variety of weights, it's best to lean toward a heavy action. A medium-weight blank simply can't deliver a cast any consequential distance.

Many anglers continue to employ fiberglass rods, although graphite and graphite composites are the rods of choice among serious surf anglers. They're stronger, lighter in weight, and capable of delivering the power needed to execute long casts.

While surf casting, you're holding and physically handling the outfit for long periods of time, casting and retrieving. Weight becomes a critical factor. Take care to purchase a rod that's comfortable to hold and not overbearing with respect to weight.

Select a heavy surf rod made with quality, lightweight components. Graphite reel seats with anodized aluminum hoods and aluminum oxide or ceramic line guides are perfect. Keep in mind that with the rods, reels, and line discussed here, there's a direct correlation between cost and quality. Take care to purchase the finest quality your purse will allow. Toward this end, a small, local tackle shop along the seacoast can often guide you in the right direction.

The majority of spinning reels designed for heavy surf spinning are capable of holding anywhere from 250 yards of 20-pound-test line to 300 yards of 30-pound monofilament. The big reels are generally more than you'll need—it's unlikely that any of the favorite four will ever clean out this quantity of line—but for heavy surf work they're favorites. Most heavy surf reels have a 4-to-1 or 4.5-to-1 gear ratio, facilitating a fast retrieve.

The multiplying reels used for high surf are generally lighter in weight than spinning reels. Line capacities range from 200 yards of 20-pound-test monofilament or braided nylon up to 350 yards of 20-pound test. Casting from the surf with a multiplying reel holding line heavier than 20-pound test is seldom practical.

Some surfcasters use lines of Spectra fiber, which enable them to use smaller reels. These microfilament lines have diameters that are only 20 percent of the diameter of monofilament line. You can use a smaller reel, but enjoy the same line capacity.

Many of the newer surf-casting reels are made of space-age composites, with graphite among the most popular because of its light weight. Quality reels are impervious to salt water and when properly cared for will give you years of dependable use.

A heavy surf outfit finds use throughout Cape Cod's outer beaches, off Montauk's heavy surf, and in the almost always rough surf of the Carolinas, where distance casting and heavy sinkers are the norm to hold the bottom.

The medium-weight surf outfit is unquestionably the most popular, versatile outfit in use along the coast.

A medium surf rod requires two hands for casting, and measures anywhere from 7 to 8 1/2 feet in overall length. Most anglers like it to have a stiff action that can punch out casts with 1/2- through 2-ounce lures. The rod still has the backbone to handle heavier lures and especially bottom rigs, where often the weight of sinker and bait reaches 4 ounces.

Most medium-weight surf reels are made with graphite frames, because it's much lighter than cast aluminum. Medium surf models handle 275 yards of 12-pound-test line or 250 yards of 15-pound test and are half the weight of the heavy surf models discussed earlier.

Some surf casters prefer a multiplying reel, and there are many models ideally suited to this fishing. The reels are made with precision-machined aluminum frames and side plates, and lightweight aluminum spools. Most of the newer models have a lever that is depressed to disengage the reel spool at the time of the cast, which is then engaged when the reel handle is turned at the time of retrieve. A level-wind mechanism ensures that the line is wound back on the spool evenly. Most multiplying reels hold approximately 250 yards of 15-pound-test monofilament.

The medium surf outfit is a favorite of South Shore anglers on Long Island and New Jersey and Delmarva casters, where sandbars often parallel the coast and the fish feed inside the bars. Long casts aren't necessary.

When light surf prevails, as is often the case during the summer months, many anglers opt to use a light, one-handed casting outfit. This is especially true when the majority of the favorite four caught in an area are schoolies.

You can walk along a prime stretch of beach with a one-handed outfit for hours, casting without fear of the fatigue encountered when using the heavier surf outfits. The light rods are generally designed to handle lures ranging from 1/4 ounce through 2 ounces.

Because of the increased popularity of one-handed rods in salt water, many companies now build small reels, both spinning and multiplying, specifically for saltwater use. A spinning reel that holds 200 yards of 10-pound-test monofilament, or about 175 yards of 12-pound-test monofilament or microfilament, is perfect for this application.

Of course, you can always opt for the popular conventional casting reel. Most saltwater bait casting reels hold 225 yards of 15-pound-test line. A conventional reel on a one-handed popping rod is a combination you can cast with all day long without tiring.

If you choose to fish with artificials, a basic rig that proves very effective is a 30- to 36-inch-long piece of 20-pound-test fluorocarbon leader material, with a small duolock snap at the end for your primary lure, and a dropper loop tied off a tiny black swivel, with a second duolock snap at the end of the 5- or 6-inch-long dropper loop for a teaser.

Mobility is paramount when fishing the surf. You want to be able to carry everything you need, yet be comfortable. Leave the tackle boxes and buckets at home; they'll just hinder your movement. There are many fine-quality shoulder bags designed expressly for surf fishermen. Select one large enough to carry the items you require, but not so large as to give you a backache.

Toward this end, veteran surfmen often carry just a small selection of proven producers, as opposed to carrying a huge selection. All too often anglers waste a lot of time and effort constantly changing lures, rather than methodically working a reliable lure through the haunts of the favorite four.

Many surfmen opt for a fly-fishing vest. While designed for fresh water, the vest has 8 or 10 roomy pockets into which you can fit all you'll need. In a size larger than you'd normally wear, the vest can be slipped over a parka or sweatshirt and will be loose enough not to encumber your casting.

Your arsenal of lures should include a surface-swimming plug, a deep diver, and a popper. While there are dozens of plug models, this basic threesome will get you through most situations. Adjust to the conditions: Use smaller sizes where bait and weather conditions dictate, and larger when targeting bigger fish.

Block tin squids, stainless-steel Hopkins NoEqls and Shorties, and chromed Ava diamond jigs should also be included as you venture to the beach. Many metal squids are now molded in the shape of various baitfish and air-brushed to exactly replicate the forage. Metals rigged with green, red, or purple tube tails with single hooks prove very effective. Shy away from those rigged with treble hooks; these hooks make unhooking the fish difficult and minimize its chance of survival if released. For ease in casting and fishing any of these lures, match the lure weight to the outfit you're using.

The float rig shown has wire through its center and is baited with a fresh mullet. It's great for bluefish because they can't bite through the wire when they strike the bait. It's a favorite with Georgia surf fishermen.

For years the bucktail jig was the standard along the beach, but with the advent of plastic bait tails, the plain leadhead jig with a plastic tail has all but replaced bucktail as the tail of choice. Here, too, carry a selection of head weights and colors that closely approximate the baitfish found in the area you plan to fish. While many of the plastic tails closely resemble sand eels, mackerel, menhaden, mullet, and other forage, there are times when hot pink receives strikes when all other colors are ignored.

A Clouser saltwater fly is the choice teaser of many veteran surfmen, because its weighted eye tends to keep the teaser extended out and away from the leader as it's retrieved. Deceivers and most other saltwater flies tied to resemble small baitfish also work well. When bluefish are plentiful, many anglers simply use a tuft of bucktail tied to a 1/0, 2/0, or 3/0 O'Shaughnessy hook, for the choppers will ruin a Clouser in short order with their sharp teeth.

The combination of a surface-swimming plug and a Clouser Minnow saltwater fly with an epoxy head is very effective when cast from the beach or jetties. The teaser can also be used with a leadhead jig or metal squid when the fish are feeding deep, and works equally well when jigged from a boat.

It's also wise to include a nail clipper, tape measure, and pair of long-nosed pliers in your vest. A rope stringer makes it much easier to carry a catch of several large fish, especially when you've walked a mile or more down the beach. And it's also a good idea to carry a small plastic bag, such as those used for groceries, into which you can place small blues, fluke, or weakfish before slipping them into the roomy rear pocket of your vest. In this way you can move about freely.

Surf-Fishing Strategies

Plan a strategy as you move out onto a stretch of beach. Daybreak and dusk, including an hour or two before and after, are times when all of the favorite four are particularly active along the beach. A good pattern is to begin with a plug and teaser combination. If the tide is high just walk, cast, and retrieve. While it's good to make long casts, every cast doesn't have to go the horizon. Remember that many of the favorite four are feeding right in the wash, often 20 or 30 feet from where you're standing.

If the tide is extremely low you can carefully wade out onto the bar; there's usually access in about the center of a bar. Exercise caution, however, because a flooding tide can rise to a depth where you have a problem returning to the beach. Fishing the water in front of the bar gives you an opportunity not afforded during high tide, when you're pushed well back on the beach and it's usually impossible to cast beyond the bar.

At midtide work the sluices behind the bars. They're often loaded with fish, as are the breaks or holes in the bar, where stripers, blues, weaks, and fluke congregate, waiting for the water depth to get to their liking.

When you fish the sluices behind the bars, the current will be flowing either to the left or right. Work this current much the same way you'd work a trout stream. Cast up into the current, and permit it to sweep your lure downcurrent as you retrieve.

Pay particular attention to movements of baitfish. Often you'll see schools of menhaden, sand eels, or other forage packed tight against the inside of the bar, or right on the edge of the drop-off along the beach. Fish an area like this methodically, using lightweight lures that will work in the thin water. If you don't receive strikes, move on and continue working the stretch of beach, but don't hesitate to return to the spot where you observed the baitfish. Eventually the favorite four will locate the bait. Perhaps an hour's difference in the tide will stimulate their interest and you'll be rewarded by a return visit.

There's no set pattern to surf fishing. You can be out in the morning and have one set of conditions, while by evening the same tide conditions will have changed markedly. Match your fishing pattern to the conditions. With a flat calm surf and air-clear water use lightweight plugs and leadheads with a light outfit. With a howling nor'easter and booming surf forget the lightweight lures. Switch over to a heavy surf outfit and 2- or 3-ounce metal squids or leadheads that you can comfortably cast into the teeth of the wind.

Successful surf fishermen have one thing in common: They go fishing whenever they have the opportunity. High tide, low tide, west wind, east wind, day or night. They get to know the drill and what to do. Success comes with getting the pulse of the surf. As you trudge over the dunes your sixth sense will tell you what lure to use and what bar may be perfect at this stage of the tide.

Get out on the beach every chance you can. Continue walking, and casting. Suddenly an electrifying jolt will be your reward. It may be any one of the favorite four. You just never know!

Casting from the surf is perhaps the most contemplative method of catching the favorite foursome. There's mile after mile of open beach, and you can repair to a quiet stretch to enjoy the sunrise—or moon-rise, as the case may be. There's the ever-changing surf, from flat calm to roaring maelstrom, from the hot sun beating down on a summer day with the prevailing afternoon southeaster to the heavens and a million stars on a cold autumn night with a northwester howling.

Of course, everyone has a personal preference. But for many, myself included, the peace and solitude of searching out a stretch of beach and studying the cuts and bar formations and being away from the crowds is paramount. During the summer months the tempera-tures are so delightful that you can often don a bathing suit and walk for hours in the gentle surf, the same surf that autumn requires waders and a warm parka to ward off the stinging onshore winds.

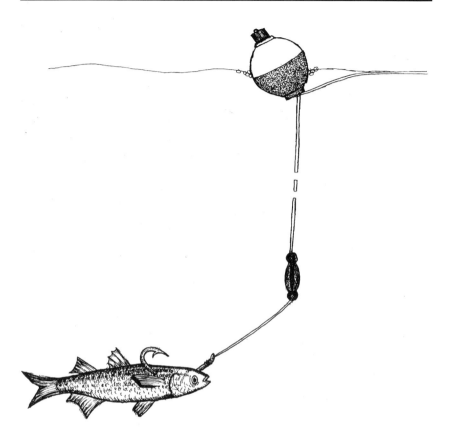

PLASTIC FLOAT RIG

The favorite four often travel at intermediate depths in the water column, and it's always wise to present baits at that level, especially when drifting or chumming, or even when other anglers are bottom fishing. The size of the float should be sufficiently large to keep from being dragged beneath the surface by the bait. If there's a swift current, a rubber-cored sinker helps keep the leader between the float and bait perpendicular to the bottom.

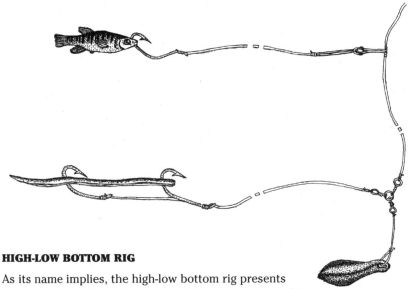

HIGH-LOW BOTTOM RIG

As its name implies, the high-low bottom rig presents
one hook high, off the bottom, and the other low, or right
on the bottom. It's especially popular with anglers targeting fluke and
weakfish, with a strip bait fished on the bottom and a live killie and strip,
or a single sandworm, fished on the high hook. The sinker weight should
be heavy enough to hold the bottom as you drift along.

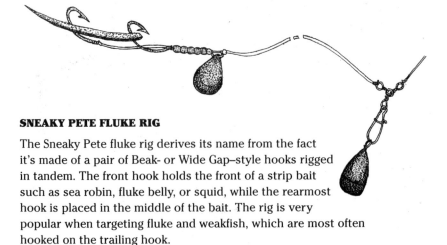

SNEAKY PETE FLUKE RIG

The Sneaky Pete fluke rig derives its name from the fact
it's made of a pair of Beak- or Wide Gap–style hooks rigged
in tandem. The front hook holds the front of a strip bait
such as sea robin, fluke belly, or squid, while the rearmost
hook is placed in the middle of the bait. The rig is very
popular when targeting fluke and weakfish, which are most often
hooked on the trailing hook.

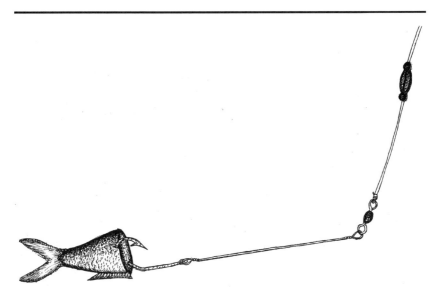

CHUNK BAIT RIG

The chunk bait rig may be used while chumming, drifting, or anchored. A tail section, head section, or chunk from the midsection of a mackerel, menhaden, or herring can be used; or try a squid head or piece of clam. Adjust the size of the rubber-cored sinker to keep the bait at the desired depth.

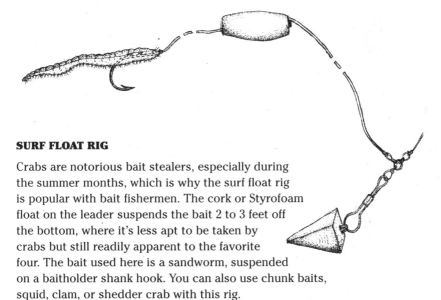

SURF FLOAT RIG

Crabs are notorious bait stealers, especially during the summer months, which is why the surf float rig is popular with bait fishermen. The cork or Styrofoam float on the leader suspends the bait 2 to 3 feet off the bottom, where it's less apt to be taken by crabs but still readily apparent to the favorite four. The bait used here is a sandworm, suspended on a baitholder shank hook. You can also use chunk baits, squid, clam, or shedder crab with this rig.

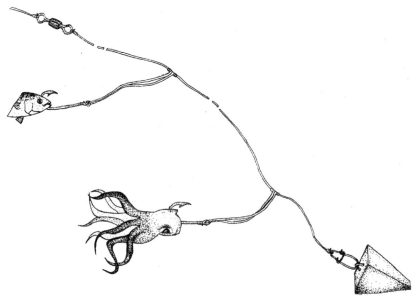

TWO-HOOK SURF RIG

The two-hook surf rig is not prone to tangling when it's cast, because the sinker carries the trailing baits during the execution of the cast. The bait hooks are looped onto a dropper loop trailing from the leader, and may be from 2 to 6 inches or more in length. You can also add a small float between the dropper loop and hook to suspend one or both baits off the bottom. Shown are the head of a mackerel and the head of a squid. A chunk of menhaden or herring, a piece of clam, or a shedder crab is also effective.

15

FISHING BRIDGES AND PIERS

Extending out into or over the water along the seacoast is a variety of man-made structures that offer fine fishing opportunities. Some of the structures, such as fishing piers, were built expressly for fishermen and located in prime habitat. Many others were built with other purposes in mind, such as the marina docks and the myriad private docks and piers that extend into bay and river waters. In many areas the canals and lagoons along the coast are lined with bulkheads, also offering access to the favorite four.

Bridges

The majority of bridges along the coast have towers holding them in place, often with accompanying icebreakers. As the tidal flow reaches the structure, rips and eddies form. Here the current is less swift, in dead spots both before the structure, where the current splits, and after the structure where it again meets.

With all these structures, it's important to determine beforehand if fishing is permitted and to abide by local regulations.

In the quiet water on both the upcurrent and downcurrent sides of the bridge, baitfish such as menhaden, spearing, sand eels, and other small fish congregate. Striped bass and weakfish congregate in the same spots, particularly when the current is running swiftly, because they expend less energy stemming the tide in this quiet water. There are times when you can observe both game fish and forage species sharing the same water in harmony. Most often it's because the heavyweights have already had their fill of the small morsels sharing a rip or eddy.

Often the stripers or weakfish in residence in an eddy will move from it to engulf a crab, shrimp, or sandworm being swept along with the current, only to return quickly to the quiet water. And on nights when there's a distinct shadow line from the lights illuminating the bridge, the fish will take up stations facing into the current, literally placing their head right at the shadow line. They stem the tide, moving to the left or right to intercept a crab or unsuspecting baitfish being swept along.

Live-bait fishing from a bridge often entails little more than tying a 30-pound-test fluorocarbon leader to the end of your line, and snelling a Beak- or Claw-style hook to the end. By slipping a single large sandworm onto a size 1/0 or 2/0 hook with a baitholder shank, you can ease it into the current, where it will swim enticingly, the eddy carrying it back and forth in a lifelike manner.

Tinker mackerel, hickory shad, menhaden, and mullet are all found in abundance in bay and river waters and can often be obtained with the aid of a cast net. Just a few of these prime baits can be kept alive in a 5-gallon pail on the bridge, enough to last an entire tide. Using either a treble or single Claw- or Beak-style hook, the bait should be hooked through the lips, nose, or eye sockets, so that as it's eased into the current it faces up into the tide.

Once it's eased into the water, you can begin by working the live bait through the eddies formed on the downcurrent side of a supporting tower. Simply keep your reel in free spool with light pressure on the line and walk back and forth along the railing, alternately relinquishing line and drifting the swimming bait back as much as a 100 feet from the bridge, then reeling back in slowly. Continue walking the bait back and forth, covering as much water as possible until a strike is received. In the rips and eddies the strikes are very deliberate. As line is pulled from the reel, point the rod in the direction of the flowing line, lock the reel into gear, and, when it comes taut, lift back smartly to set the hook.

On some long, low-level bridges you can walk great distances, swimming the bait through the many eddies behind the supporting towers and the swift currents that form between them.

JIGS AND PLUGS

Leadhead jigs with plastic tails or bucktail jigs and plugs are the prime lures in the arsenal of the bridge fisherman.

Where stripers and weakfish are the major species in residence, the leadhead jig with a plastic tail finds favor. If there's an abundance of bluefish in the waters surrounding a favorite span, it's simply very costly to use the plastic tails—the blues will bite through them in an instant. Then the bucktail jig becomes the lure of choice. While bluefish teeth can destroy bucktail, it does last longer than plastic.

It's wise to carry a selection of weights, with 1/4-ounce, 1/2-ounce, and 1-ounce models ideal for slow-water conditions when you want to work the lure near the surface. Tuck in a couple of 2- and 3-ounce models for situations where the tide is running swiftly and you want to probe the depths.

The lighter leadheads work very effectively when cast up into the current flowing toward the bridge and then worked back to you with a whip retrieve, causing the jig to dart ahead and falter, much like a struggling baitfish being swept along by the tide. Also cast at a 45-degree angle and work the jig across the current, again using a whip retrieve. Both techniques are especially effective at night when stripers and weaks are in the shadows, facing the shadow line and bright lights as food is swept toward them.

On the downcurrent side of a bridge it's often best to cast parallel to the bridge, letting the jig settle as it's swept along with the tide through the rips and eddies. Here, too, a whip retrieve works very well, although on occasion a slow, steady retrieve brings strikes.

While lightweight jigs will bring strikes from surface-feeding fish, there are often times when the fish are hugging the bottom. To reach them you've got to move up to the heavier lures, those 2- and 3-ounce models. Use the same approach, casting both up into the current and down, permitting the jig to reach the bottom, and then literally bouncing it along the bottom. Often strikes will be received at the end of a swing, as the current lifts the lure off the bottom.

A strip of pork rind enhances the action of a bucktail jig, and you'd be well served to use it while bridge fishing. Likewise, try a teaser fished 24 to 36 inches ahead of the primary lure. The teaser will often draw strikes when the fish are feeding on grass shrimp, tiny crabs, spearing, sand eels, and other tiny forage.

Plugs can also be employed very effectively from bridges. Some of the most exciting fishing you'll experience comes from working a surface-swimming plug through the same water described earlier. Often there's no sign of bait or fish; your small plug appears to be simply struggling to maintain itself in the current, when out of the depths a big striper, blue, or weak will boil to the surface to strike.

The key in fishing a surface swimmer is to use a very slow retrieve—barely turn the reel handle. This results in a lazy, side-to-side action as the plug is pushed by the current and then stems the tide in a rip or eddy. Some anglers just cast out from a bridge and walk back and forth, permitting the current pushing against the plug to give it an enticing action.

Casting up into or across the current is also very effective. Reel just fast enough to keep the slack out of the line as the plug swims toward the shadow line (if you're fishing at night). Often you can observe a big striper or weak streak out 10 feet or more from the shadow line to crash down on the plug.

By far the best surface-swimming plugs are those with a nearly vertical metal lip and made of wood. These float no matter how fast or slow you retrieve them, which is the key. Color doesn't seem to matter; the action is what attracts the fish and draws strikes.

You can also use a deep-diving plug, such as a mirror-type or rattle plug, to probe the depths much as you would a bucktail or leadhead jig. Neither of these plug types has a lip; they can be retrieved slow, fast, or with a whip retrieve, causing them to dart ahead and falter, much like a baitfish struggling in the current.

Piers and Docks

Many of these same techniques—for both natural baits and lures—can be employed from piers and docks, especially those located in rivers where there's a strong current. The conditions here are very much like those encountered while bridge fishing.

On piers and docks you'll also experience the same conditions at night, for often the dock lights will result in a shadow line. Fish take up stations in the shadows to wait for a meal.

The key in fishing lures from the many types of structures discussed in this chapter is not to become a mechanical caster. All too often anglers stand in one spot, casting over and over, reeling mechanically with little regard to lure action or current. It's important to vary your lures. Sometimes a surface-swimming plug will bring explosive strikes, particularly on slack water. When the tide is roaring and the fish are hugging the bottom, a heavy leadhead cast up and across current, then permitted to settle and bounce on the bottom, will bring strikes when a plug swimming on the surface would be ignored.

Still, while it's good to change lures, this can be overdone. Some anglers carry a shoulder bag of lures and are constantly changing. A far better approach is to determine which two or three lures are best suited to making a good presentation from the surface to the bottom, and building confidence in those lures. In so doing, you master the feel that each lure is working properly. Invariably your catch will be enhanced.

RIGS

In chapter 12 you'll find a discussion of the breeches buoy rig, which very effectively fishes live bait in the surf. The breeches buoy rig is equally effective when fishing from piers and docks, where you're trying to place the bait in a specific location.

The bulkheads that line many waterways, such as inlets, canals, and lagoons, also present opportunities for both live bait and lures. With live bait you can use much the same technique employed by bridge fishermen, walking the bait along the bulkhead.

A particularly effective rig for keeping live bait such as sandworms, soft crabs, or small baitfish at intermediate levels is to use a float. Begin by doubling the terminal end of your line with a surgeon's loop. Then use a 3- to 4-foot-long piece of fluorocarbon leader material and tie it to the double line formed by the loop with a surgeon's knot. Snell or tie the bait hook of your choice in an appropriate size to the terminal end of the leader; Beak and Claw styles are ideal.

Several types of floats are very popular for this type of fishing. The plastic float with a spring-activated snap enables you to snap it in place on the line, regulating the depth at which the bait is fished.

Styrofoam floats are also effective. These are slid onto the line and held in place with a pin that is in turn inserted into the float.

Some anglers prefer a sliding float, which enables you to cast out the bait with ease. You must first determine the depth you wish to fish your bait, and then tie a double overhand knot at that spot. Next a small button—of the size you'd find on a man's shirt—is slipped onto the line, followed by a plastic, Styrofoam, or cork float with a hole

Bulkheads such as this line many waterways along the seacoast. They provide easy access to fishable water, enabling anglers to score with the favorite four.

through the middle. The rig is completed with a leader and hook as described earlier. A small rubber-cored sinker is slipped onto the leader approximately 12 inches from the bait.

With this rig you can bait up with a sandworm or mackerel and reel the knot through the guides of your rod, with the float and button sliding down the line toward sinker and bait. This enables you to cast the rig to a desired spot. There the sinker will cause the bait to settle into the depths, and the button and float will slide up the line until the knot stops the button.

This rig works very well where you want to always fish the bait at a specific depth. If you want to change depths, you've got to reposition the placement of the knot.

The float and natural bait combination is especially effective in canals or other constricted waterways in spots where a swift current is slowed. As the tide slackens the favorite four become active and move about in search of food, vacating holding spots in holes, along ridges, and in the rips and eddies where there's minimal current during the height of the tide.

Chapter 12 describes a very effective bottom rig for fluke. The two-hook strip bait rig with a small Colorado spinner is extremely effective when fishing from all of the structures discussed in this chapter, including bridges, piers, docks, and bulkheads.

A light popping outfit and a bottom rig with a combination live killie and strip bait accounted for this catch of fluke from a pier on the South Carolina coast.

When using this rig in these waterways it's important to cover as much bottom as possible. It's a mistake to stand in one spot casting out and retrieving the strip bait rig over and over, because the bait continues to cover the same bottom.

The best approach from almost all of these structures is to begin with a short cast up into the current. Slowly retrieve the rig and then extend your next cast by 5 or 10 feet, which brings the bait over an entirely new stretch of bottom. Keep extending the distance of your casts, as far as practical. Once you're sure you've saturated the bottom with your presentation, then walk 15 or 20 feet from where you were standing and begin all over again. This method requires a lot of casting and concentration, and you'll do a lot of walking. At day's end the reward is invariably a good catch.

Fishing for the favorite four from piers, bridges, docks, and bulkheads is relaxing, relatively safe, and ideal for the shore-based angler who finds the challenge of jetties and surf more than he wishes to undertake.

There's a lot more to mastering the skills of presenting lures and baits from structures than meets the eye. As with all of the techniques discussed throughout this book, by studying the water and learning the habits of the fish that frequent a particular waterway, you'll enjoy each and every tide change along the seacoast.

Jim Carey holds aloft a 12-pound striper on a Boga Gripper that was just landed by Tom Shilen. It was hooked sight-casting a Clouser minnow on the North Shore of Long Island, and is the nearest thing you'll find to bonefishing.

IV
Using Fly-Casting Tackle

Striped bass are easily immobilized by using your thumb and forefinger to hold their lower jaw. This bass was released moments after the fly was removed.

16

FLY FISHING FROM BOAT AND BEACH

The use of fly-fishing tackle when seeking the favorite four has grown tremendously in recent years. Fly casters fishing from both shore and boat have realized the great potential of the long rod and the exciting challenges it presents under a wide variety of fishing situations.

The techniques discussed in the various chapters of this book are by and large the most effective when seeking a particular species with multiplying and spinning tackle. Under some circumstances, however, the long rod can be equally effective. Also, and important too, there's a mystique to fly fishing that tends to hook you once you become involved. There's something fascinating in tying on a nearly weightless tuft of feathers and bucktail and executing a cast that drops it precisely on target, often 50 feet or more from where you're standing.

Fly-Casting Tackle and Techniques

Fly fishing is a challenge. You've got to acquire the skills of casting while also mastering the use of a variety of fly lines and learning how to effectively give action to the fly to coax strikes. It's not something that's done overnight, but often develops into a lifelong pursuit.

Perhaps the single most important difference between fly casting and other types of casting rests in precisely what is cast. A spinning or multiplying reel casts the lure, such as a plug or jig; it provides the weight that takes it to the target. With fly fishing, the fly, which for all practical purposes has no weight, is not cast; the fly line does have weight, however, and this is what actually carries the leader and fly to the target.

Saltwater fly fishing for stripers, weakfish, bluefish, and fluke has drawn many freshwater anglers to coastal waters. They quickly find that by moving up from the 4- and 5-weight outfits used for trout and panfish, they can experience exciting sport with an 8- to 10-weight outfit designed to handle salt water's heavier fly lines and larger flies.

The key in saltwater fly fishing is beginning with a properly balanced rod, reel, line, and leader. Fly-fishing tackle is rated with a number system tied to the weight of the tackle—more specifically, to the weight of the fly line. For purposes of seeking the big four species, the choice of most anglers ranges from an 8- to a 10-weight. A 9-weight outfit is a good choice for an angler entering this domain.

Quality tackle is important in all types of saltwater fishing, but it's especially important in fly casting. The weight of the outfit plays an important role: You want one light enough to cast for hours without fatigue. Reels made of cast aluminum with finely tuned drag systems and graphite rods weighing perhaps half as much as fiberglass make good choices.

For years anglers had to employ as many as four or more types of fly line to suit the variety of conditions they encounter. These included floating-tip lines, slow-sinking tip, moderate-sinking tip, and fast-sinking tip. Many anglers actually carried as many as four complete fly-fishing outfits with them so as to be prepared for any contingency.

Today anglers are afforded the opportunity to use a single fly line with four changeable tips. Each tip section offers attached loops for quick changing, a small-diameter running line, and an extra-stiff braided monofilament core to cast large flies and ease casting during the windy conditions so often encountered along the seacoast.

LEADERS

A key part of any fly-fishing outfit is the leader. The fly line is used to execute the cast and carry the fly to the target; a tapered leader becomes an extension of the fly line. Properly tapered, the leader turns the fly over so, at the completion of the cast, the line and leader lie straight.

While many tapered fly leaders are made of monofilament, you'd be best served to use those made of fluorocarbon, for its refractive index is such that it's virtually invisible in the water. This give you a distinct advantage, particularly when fishing for stripers and weakfish, both of which are found on the flats, in very clear, shallow water.

The majority of tapered leaders range from 8 to 10 feet in length, with three or four sections tapering from tests of 30-, to 20-, to 16- or 12-pound tippet. The leader sections are joined using a blood knot; a uni-knot or improved clinch knot attaches the fly. A surgeon's end loop may be used to loop the leader to the loop at the end of the fly line. A shorter leader, in the 6-foot range, is adequate for most saltwater situations. A good rule of thumb is to employ those with a 12- through 16-

pound-test tippet. Often the favorite four will engulf a fly and inhale it, resulting in the tippet being abused via teeth or the roughness of the fish's jaw, making it advantageous to use the heavier tippet.

When you're targeting bluefish specifically, you should use tapered leaders with 4 to 8 inches of lightweight stainless-steel wire shock tippets. These have retwistable haywire connections, making fly changing easy and preventing the blues from biting through the leader.

Many fly casters employ the new, state-of-the-art titanium wire for leader material when targeting bluefish. Titanium wire can be tied using an improved clinch knot to fasten the lure to the leader. An Albright knot is used to attach the titanium wire to the tippet end of the tapered leader. These are the only two knots effective with titanium wire.

There are many manufacturers that specialize in fly-fishing tackle, and you should take your time to examine the wide range available before making a selection; it can make a world of difference in your enjoyment on the water. Many fly-fishing tackle shops permit you to try casting with an outfit before you commit to purchasing it. Take advantage of this opportunity so you have a comfort level with a particular combination of rod, reel, line, and leader.

A soft, lifeless rod with a heavy reel, inferior-quality fly line, and poorly tapered leader results in fatigue and an inability to cast effortlessly. With a balanced outfit and a powerful graphite rod, on the other hand, you can learn to execute casts of sufficient distance to catch the favorite four after just a few hours of practice casting.

FLY PATTERNS

As is the case with plugs, spoons, leadhead jigs, and diamond jigs, in fly fishing there are myriad fly patterns from which to choose. Some are tied to resemble grass shrimp, others to look like a crab. There are those that resemble squid, spearing, menhaden, mackerel, mullet, rainfish, and a variety of other forage species. Within the framework of the species mentioned, each fly tyer adds his personality to a given pattern. The more you look at fly patterns, the more confusing it can be; even with respect to sizes, you'll find flies ranging from size 4 to size 5/0. All have their place in the scheme of things. Still, you needn't carry a fly box loaded with hundreds of patterns. Instead, carefully select a handful of proven patterns and learn how to use them. You'll catch more fish than the angler who changes flies every couple of casts.

The key in fly selection rests with having a nominal number of patterns. It's a matter of disciplining yourself and selecting the patterns that most closely resemble the forage that predominates in the area you plan to fish. As I was preparing this book, I asked world-renowned saltwater fly tyer Bob Popovics to provide input on the selection of flies that have produced consistent results over a period of many years.

He basically narrowed the selection to 15 patterns, holding to the size that most nearly imitates the size of the baitfish normally encountered. His selection for the inshore middle and Northeast Atlantic fishery and the species targeted here includes: Cotton Candy, 3-D FLEYE, Menhaden, Lefty's Deceiver, Purple Bunny, Bend Back, Clouser Minnow, Wide Side Peanut Bunker, Jiggy, Bob's Banger, Merkin Crab, Pink Shrimp, Honey Blonde, and Multi Wing Streamer. Armed with this selection, Bob's prepared for every bait contingency, with the offering covering the water column from top to bottom.

I've narrowed my own selection to just a handful of flies. My fly pouch includes the Clouser, Lefty's Deceiver, White Marabou, Menhaden, Top Water Slider, Popovics Silver Popper, Grass Shrimp, Surf Candy, and Crab Fly. Some might argue that it's better to have a large selection, but switching patterns often takes precious time when the fish are feeding. Worth noting is that all of the favorite four will nearly always take a fly that comes close to resembling the forage they're feeding on.

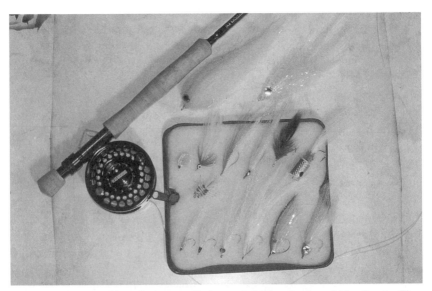

Bob Popovics, one of America's great fly tyers, tied this selection of 15 saltwater flies. With these flies and a 9- or 10-weight fly-casting outfit you'll catch the favorite four.

Given the choice, if you had to choose just one fly for all species, all conditions, and all sizes of bait, the Clouser Deep Swimming Minnow with an epoxy head, tied on a 1/0 through 3/0 hook, would be an excellent choice. It casts well and can be fished high in the water column by promptly stripping, or permitted to settle into the depths before retrieving. It has large eyes and a light dressing of bucktail and Mylar. Choose colors to match the baitfish on hand: brown and white with gold Mylar when sand eels are plentiful, chartreuse and white with silver Mylar when spearing are the bait of choice, and other colors to simulate the bait normally found where you plan to fish. Once you gain experience, you'll find that you seldom change flies during a day, or week, or more; you'll stick with the fly you're most comfortable with and that consistently produces results for you.

In other chapters there are discussions of using a teaser ahead of a primary lure, either casting from shore or jigging from a boat. Few people realize that a teaser can also prove deadly when fly fishing. Trout fishermen have for years employed a dry fly as the primary lure, with a wet fly or nymph several feet ahead of it, fished off a dropper loop as a teaser. The same works well in salt water. Simply tie a dropper loop onto your leader, then loop on a 6-inch-long leader with a Honey Blonde, Marabou, or Multi Wing Streamer. You'll be pleasantly surprised. Fish frequently strike the teaser, and sometimes you'll even score with a doubleheader!

The final item you'll need for fly fishing in salt water is a stripping basket. There are a number of models available, ranging from a kitchen dishpan with a belt attached to it to canvas models that fold up when not in use. They're helpful while fishing from both boat and shore. The stripping basket is placed at your side or in front of you, held in position via a belt. When you strip the fly line during the retrieve, you store it neatly in the basket. It saves the line from getting tangled around your feet while fishing from the surf, or from getting fouled on the cleats and other accoutrements found on the typical fishing boat.

Let it be said from the outset that there's no "perfect" method of fly fishing. If boat fishing is your forte, then so be it. If it's fishing from the shore, then by all means enjoy it. Those who fish from boat and shore, both enjoy using what many feel is the ultimate tool, the fly rod.

Fly fishing from boats on the open water of the ocean, bays, and sounds is spectacular sport when bluefish and striped bass are herding baitfish on the surface. When the fish are up they're easily located, because seagulls arrive from miles around to join in the feast of the helpless fry being herded from below. This is exciting fishing, with the bass and blues so caught up in chasing the bait that they'll readily respond to a fly.

It's important to approach a school of surface-feeding fish quietly and from the side; this way the helmsman of a small boat can maintain steerage into the wind and current. The fly fisherman can position himself in the bow and be able to cast his fly into the feeding maelstrom.

You've got to get within casting range, and for most newcomers this means 40- to 60-foot casts. While much of the action appears in the middle of the schools of menhaden, spearing, rainfish, or other forage, quite often there are bass and blues prowling along the perimeter of the school. Make your casts as close to the feeding fish as possible, but strip the fly right back to the boat before lifting it to make another cast. Often strikes will come at the last moment, when a game fish sees your fly as a small bait leaving the main school and presenting an easy target.

When the fish are on top a popper or slider works well, but as noted in earlier chapters, for every fish you see on top there are hundreds below. Fishing top-water flies is unquestionably the most exciting, as the fish attack the fly in a feeding frenzy. The key is using a floating-tip line and sliding the fly across the surface, or working the popper to make it pop and gurgle much like a small fish struggling on the surface.

Keeping a tight line and consistent pattern is important, and by all means don't hesitate during the retrieve. Some anglers use their left hand to strip into the stripping basket. Many anglers have adopted a technique of executing their cast, then quickly placing the rod under their left armpit and using a two-handed, hand-over-hand stripping retrieve, resulting in a steadier and faster retrieve.

There are times, however, when the surface flies don't produce as you would suspect, and it pays to put on a fly that will probe the depths. The Clouser Minnow, Half & Half, and Deceiver patterns regularly produce fine results. All of these patterns come close to resembling the multitude of bait the fish are attacking.

As noted in earlier chapters, chumming proves very effective in attracting all of the favorite four within range of natural baits and lures. A well-established chum line also can provide bonanza fishing to the fly caster, for it brings all four of our targeted species within range.

Indeed, it's not unusual when several anglers are fishing a chum line to have some using natural baits or lures. The fly caster should stand unobtrusively to the side, where his backcast doesn't interfere with anyone. By casting at an angle across the current, permitting the fly to settle, and then beginning an erratic retrieve you can be assured of fast action, often scoring more strikes with flies than by the traditional method of bait and other lures.

When fish are in a chum line they'll often hold in the midrange of the water column. A fast-sinking tip will get your fly down quickly. This is where the Clouser Minnow, Lefty's Deceiver, Half & Half, and especially a small Pink Shrimp excel.

FISHING SHADOW LINES

Practically every inshore waterway along the middle and Northeast Atlantic coast has illuminated bridges, docks, bulkheads, and marinas where a shadow line falls on the water. Striped bass and weakfish are known for their habit of stemming the tide here, facing into the current as they wait for food to be swept their way.

Shadow lines provide exciting opportunities for fly casters. The helmsman can position the boat off to the side of where the fish are located, enabling the caster to shoot his fly line upcurrent or across and strip the fly back within the range of the fish holding in the current.

Not to be forgotten is probing the rips and eddies that form around these same structures. The current is less severe in the eddies, and a striper or weakfish can take up a leisurely station, simply darting out to engulf any unsuspecting crab, shrimp, or baitfish being carried along by the current.

At night when you're fishing the shadow line, rips, and eddies around bridges, alternate between surface flies like the Top Water Slider and Popovics Popper, and deep probers like the Clouser, Lefty's Deceiver, and Pink Shrimp. If menhaden and herring fingerlings are plentiful, use a full-bodied Menhaden pattern and just let it slide along slowly in the current, its body breathing during the retrieve. A Crab Fly will entice a strike if you cast across current and dead drift, with no drag on the fly. This is much the way a calico or blue crab would swim and drift with the current.

SIGHT CASTING

The nearest thing to bonefishing found along the middle and Northeast Atlantic coast is being poled along the shallows of coastal bays and sounds and sight casting to cruising striped bass, weakfish, and bluefish. The 2- to 5-foot-deep shallows adjacent to the shoreline of almost every coastal bay and sound are expressways for these species. Baitfish such as spearing, sand eels, menhaden, herring, and other small forage generally seek the sanctuary of the "thin" water along the shoreline, often moving over the clear sand in depths of just a few inches.

Game fish know this, and they'll often cruise along the shallows, that range of water up to 100 feet from shore. By using a push pole to quietly move a flat skiff along the shallows, an angler can comfortably stand on the bow. Polarized sunglasses reduce glare and let you look into the water, where you can readily spot the fish as they cruise between you and the shore in search of a meal.

Unlike bonefish or permit, which move very slowly as they root in the bottom, stripers, blues, and weaks are often moving swiftly. This requires constant attention and immediate response to get the fly in the air and to make a presentation that intercepts the moving fish. Sometimes it's single fish you'll be targeting, but it may be a pod of six or more fish moving together.

The key is getting the line in the air and, with minimal false casting, making a presentation to the moving fish. Get the fly into the water and moving into the range of vision of the moving fish. Steady and even is essential, with your rod tip low and pointed in the direction the line is lying. Sometimes a fast retrieve works best, and other times a slow one. Avoid slack in your line as you're stripping; this causes a dead spot and the fly begins to settle, no longer resembling a morsel of food.

Windy conditions often hamper fly casters who sight cast to cruising fish—it's hard to see them. Often during the summer months the winds come up as temperatures rise during the day. The early-morning hours, once the sun gets high in the sky and before it becomes hot, invariably produce the best opportunities.

FLY FISHING FOR FLUKE

Fluke are bottom feeders for the most part, and you wouldn't suspect that they'd readily take a fly—but they do. The key to effectively presenting a fly and consistently catching summer flounder is fishing the shallow flats of rivers and bays. On a flooding tide flatfish vacate the channels, moving onto the flats where the water is often only a couple of feet deep. They move right along the shoreline, especially those shorelines with abundant marsh grass, because grass shrimp, crabs, killies, spearing, and other forage seek what little sanctuary this grass offers. The flatfish often bury themselves in the mud or soft sand lining the banks, darting out when an unsuspecting meal happens by.

Drifting or poling across the shallows permits you to cover a lot of water. The fishing takes patience and lots of blind casting, for most often you won't see the fish. Occasionally, however, you'll see splashes as fluke swim off the bottom to engulf spearing or other fry from the surface.

A Clouser Deep Swimming Minnow, Mark's Prober, or Lefty's Deceiver fly tied on a 1/0 hook is a good choice, using the same colors discussed

Called fluke through most of their range and flounder in the South, they frequent the shallows and make great sport on a fly rod. A Clouser Minnow saltwater fly proved the downfall of this beauty.

earlier. Just use a comfortable 40- to 50-foot cast, permit the fly to settle, and begin an irregular strip retrieve. This causes the fly to dart ahead, falter, and move ahead again, much like a baitfish swimming in the shallows. Fluke are very aggressive and will move swiftly to catch a fly being stripped even at fast speed. Sometimes they'll chase the fly right to the surface, as you're about to pick it up to prepare for another cast.

The Pink Shrimp fly, which closely resembles a grass shrimp, is an excellent choice, as is a Crab Fly. Both shrimp and crabs move in the shallows at a leisurely pace. Vary the speed of your retrieve for best results. The key to this type of blind fishing is covering a lot of bottom with your offering. With wind or current propelling you, or poling the boat in the shallow water, you'll seldom bring your fly across the same bottom twice.

Once you begin to hook fish, take note of the type of bottom or conditions where the strikes are being received. At times the flounder will be tight to the marsh grass, sometimes over shallow weed beds, or often just buried in the soft mud or sand or open bottom. Try all of these conditions, and once you've scored, concentrate your efforts on the most productive.

At the very bottom of the tide, when the flats you've been fishing are devoid of water, you can probe the depths of channels adjacent to the flats. This takes a great deal of patience, for in water 6 to 8 feet deep it takes a long while for a fly to settle to the bottom. It also takes a great deal of patience to continue to work it along the bottom.

Some successful fly casters cast out, let their sinking line take the fly to the bottom, and then permit it to drift along, carried by the drift of the boat. Just lifting the rod tip causes the fly to lift from the bottom and settle back down, much like a small fish, shrimp, or crab being carried by the current. Don't be surprised if you hook an occasional weakfish, striper, or blue using this technique.

The Saltwater Fly Rodder

There was a time not too many years ago when you seldom observed a fly caster fishing the surf, or casting from a jetty or bank of a coastal river. All that's changed; fly fishing has come into vogue along the middle and Northeast Atlantic shoreline.

Throughout the summer many anglers don a bathing suit, strap on a stripping basket, and probe the shallow reaches of bays and rivers with their long rod and tuft of feathers or bucktail. They score remarkably well, for often their offering reaches fish that are in the shallows and beyond the practical depth range of boatmen.

The same holds true along the surf and from coastal jetties. Enjoying the warmth of summer and walking barefoot in the surf and hooking all four species is perhaps the easiest fishing of all, and you can participate whenever time permits. Here, too, the fly fisherman is placing his offering in areas an average of 40 to 60 feet from where he's standing. Boatmen can't reach these areas, and most conventional surf casters are using larger lures and baits. This gives the shore-based caster a decided advantage, for he can reach fish that others cannot.

Still, fly casting from shore has certain limitations. An onshore wind and rough surf may hold dividends for the conventional caster, but they result in a virtually impossible situation for the long-rod devotee. Where a conventional caster can execute extremely long casts to reach out to feeding stripers, blues, and weaks, the casting range of the fly rodder is limited.

As a result it's necessary to work around the weather. Often it's wise to go forth prepared with multiplying or spinning tackle, and to hold the fly rod in reserve until the right conditions are available.

Of course, as the temperatures wane in autumn, it becomes necessary to don waders—as is the case in spring when water temperatures are still cold. Other than waders, a fly vest to hold your gear, a miner's neck light if you plan to fish in the dark, and a stripping basket to avoid tangled line, all you need is the ambition to walk along and present your offerings.

There isn't a single stretch of surf within the range of the favorite four where you can't catch them on a fly rod. The single most important thing to remember is that the majority of the fish you're targeting are often feeding within a rod's length of where you're standing. That means standing on the beach, not in the water. Unquestionably the single biggest mistake made by most newcomers to fly fishing is that they tend to wade, which results in their being in the water at the very spot where the fish would normally be feeding!

Resist the urge to wade. Instead, concentrate your casts so they're effectively retrieved right onto the beach. This may mean standing back 5 or 10 feet from the water's edge, executing your cast, and, with tip held low, stripping your fly back in until it literally slides up on the sand.

In earlier chapters there are detailed descriptions of sandbar formations, breaks in the bars, deep holes between the bars, and the sluices inside the bars. It's the water inside the bars that often holds the bait and, in turn, the fish. These are also the spots most easily accessed by surf fly casters.

On sloping beaches without a bar formation there's often a drop-off, where the water suddenly has a nearly vertical drop of several feet. Baitfish often seek the sanctuary of the "thin water" between the sand and the drop-off, and game fish regularly move in from the deep to attack menhaden, spearing, sand eels, rainfish, and other forage.

It's also along this thin water, and in the shallow sluices inside the bar formations, where the action of the waves turns over and exposes surf clams, calico and blue crabs, and sand bugs. The favorite four know this and regularly move in water so shallow it surprises the newcomer.

Indeed, it would serve you well to reconnoiter an area you plan to fish during a low tide, preferably shortly after daybreak, a time of peak activity for the favorite four. Study the water and visually probe the shallows for signs of bait and the fish stalking it. Often you'll be surprised at the activity taking place so close to where you're standing.

FISHING GROINS

The many rock and wooden groins extending into the water in bays, rivers, and the open ocean also provide sanctuary for a variety of foods sought by the favorite four. It's especially noticeable at low tide, where you can sit and watch crabs scurry about among the submerged rocks, or baitfish swimming in the tight pockets and tidal pools formed by the ebbing tide. Stripers and weaks often take up stations along the perimeter, waiting for an opportunity to engulf an unsuspecting prey. Fluke also bury themselves in the sand, watching and waiting for a morsel of food to come within range.

While fishing from rock piles is difficult, some fly fishermen manage quite well, especially with calm wind and tidal conditions that enable them to position themselves for ease in casting. A word of caution, however: Don't walk on wood or rock groins and attempt to fly fish without adequate footwear, such as golf cleats or Korkers, to keep you from losing your footing on slippery rocks.

Getting the Fly to the Fish

Although the majority of fish you're apt to hook while fly fishing from the surf will strike flies worked at intermediate depths or along the bottom with a moderate-sinking or fast-sinking line, there are times when a floating tip has its advantages. This is particularly true when rainfish, menhaden, and spearing are huddling in tight-packed schools on the surface. Often the favorite four will herd the bait, working along the perimeter of the school, attacking any stragglers.

When baitfish are on top and you observe stripers, blues, or weaks breaking among them, with baitfish leaping into the air, it presents a perfect opportunity for a floating-tip line and a fly that will work on the surface. The Popovics Popper works much like a popping plug, popping and gurgling as it's retrieved, resembling a struggling baitfish. Often it brings immediate strikes. A Black Slider, which, as its name implies, slides through the water on the surface, resembles a submarine as it pushes water aside while being stripped forward. It's deadly when the fish are herding bait, as is a Surf Candy.

Worth repeating is the fact it's not necessary to struggle to make long casts. The most successful surf fly casters are those who methodically work a stretch of beach. Make a cast, or two or three, if a spot looks promising, then walk several feet and repeat. Don't hesitate to walk 1/2 mile or more of beach. Often the fish are on the move, frequently with no signs whatsoever. Suddenly they spot your fly, and you've got instant action!

Still another spot that warrants attention is wherever a creek or rivulet enters a bay or river. On an ebbing tide bait is carried toward the mouth, for often the shallow creeks run dry at the bottom of the tide. Stripers, weakfish, and flounder set up stations, feeding on the grass shrimp, crabs, and baitfish carried their way. Position yourself at the mouth and cast your offering up and across the current, permitting it to be swept along naturally, slowly stripping as it reaches the end of its swing. It's at the completion of the swing, as the Clouser or Deceiver suddenly lifts off the bottom and appears to be struggling against the tide, that strikes are received. A popper also brings strikes in the thin water of the creek.

Although little has been written about it, fishing with a fly rod at night is an extremely effective technique. The only extra equipment you'll require is a miner's headlamp to secure around your neck. With little wind, the water takes on a slick calm. You can often hear baitfish fluttering on the surface, sometimes thousands of them packed tightly against the beach, for they know if they venture from the shallows they risk attack.

Employ the same techniques you'd use during daytime hours. Be conscious of dock or streetlights providing illumination of the area, for the lights often attract bait, and in turn the game fish. The full moon often impacts the fishing. Its moon tides and brightness provide an eerie combination as you probe the haunts of your favorite four.

All too often newcomers to saltwater fly fishing are held spellbound by casters who regularly lay out 100 feet of line. As a result, many casters fall into the bad habit of furiously working to cast a long distance. This isn't necessary for the species included in this book— or most species, for that matter. Master the skill to regularly cast 40 to 60 feet of line with ease. If you're comfortable doing this, you'll catch more than your share of fish, simply because your fly is in the strike zone more often than that of the long-distance caster.

Also remember that the fish you're seeking are often right at the water's edge. They're working the thin water, the drop-offs, and along the edge of the rocks. Don't make the mistake made by so many of wading right into the area where the fish are apt to be feeding. Stand back and strip the fly right onto the beach. The strikes are often so close as to startle you.

The personal satisfaction of catching the favorite four while fly casting is difficult to beat. Everything depends on you: The selection of a fly, the presentation, and the satisfaction of landing great game fish on an outfit that weighs but ounces. Once you've tried it, it can become a lifelong addiction.

V
Enjoying YOUR Catch

June Rosko's recipes result in a delightful seafood dinner when the catch has been properly handled and cleaned.

CLEANING YOUR CATCH

Few would dispute that a delicious seafood dinner is a treat that's difficult to beat. Still, there are many people who don't care for seafood, simply because it tastes and smells "fishy." Indeed, how often have you smelled fish cooking and practically gagged from the odor? Even in reputable seafood restaurants many have had the same experience!

The keys to enjoying a quality fish dinner of any of the favorite four are proper handling and cooking of the fish, from the moment it's caught right up until it's put on your plate. A lot can, and often does, go wrong along the way.

After the Fish Is Caught

Let's take it from the beginning—the moment you land your favorite catch, be it a weakfish in a coastal estuary, a striper from the crashing surf, a bluefish on an offshore lump, or a summer flounder coaxed from a shallow flat. First, bleed the fish. This is simple to do and adds to the quality of the fish, yet the majority of anglers fail to do it. Insert a sharp knife into the side of the fish just behind the pectoral fin. Do this while the fish is still alive and you'll immediately draw blood; the heart will literally pump all the blood from the fish.

If the fishing is fast and furious, it's easy to understand that you may not want to take the time to clean the fish. It is, however, important that the fish be gutted as soon after as it's landed as is possible. This is especially true with weakfish and bluefish.

It's not unusual to observe people cleaning bluefish when they return late in the day—when the fish have already begun to decompose. The stomach section of the fish is often so soft from lying in a hot fish box that you could push your finger through the meat. The acids in the stomach coupled with mossbunker can result in a combination that ruins what could have been an excellent piece of fish.

Gutting your catch is easy. Do so as soon as there's a lull in the action. Use a razor-sharp knife. Make a cut from the front of the fish just under the gills and continue back to the vent. Cleanly cut the throat, and finally cut the vent tube; you can now remove and discard the entire stomach. A last step is to cut away the gills, as these too can cause a fish's quality to deteriorate. You can use seawater to clean out the stomach cavity, and it's ready to go on ice.

The next important consideration is getting the fish out of the air and onto ice. To this day many anglers head out without adequate ice, or any ice at all for that matter. They relegate the catch to lying on the deck, or in a 5-gallon pail or burlap sack. Exposure to air, even in cold weather, causes the fish to dry out and begin to deteriorate. Worse still is the common practice of filling a 5-gallon bucket with water and putting the fish in it, to literally cook as the day progresses.

While it may be inconvenient to carry a big cooler with you, whether aboard a party, charter, or private boat, it's the only way to go. Stock up with plenty of ice. Block ice is good, but shaved ice or cubed ice is better. Lay the fish on the ice, or better still bury it in the ice, even filling the stomach cavity with ice, so it immediately goes to work cooling down the fish.

Almost all coolers have a drain hole, and it's important to keep it open so that as the ice melts the water can drain away. You don't want

The author fillets his fluke as soon as he returns to dockside. Keeping the catch on ice as soon as it's caught and cleaning promptly are the keys to fine-flavored seafood dinners.

your fish lying in water at the bottom of the cooler; the water, even though chilled, will cause the fish to soften and deteriorate.

Surf fishermen should follow the same procedure just outlined, but of course won't have a cooler and ice available. Instead, after you've bled and gutted your catch, then washed the stomach cavity, bury the fish in moist sand, making certain it's above the high-water mark. This easy step is far better than strewing your catch on the sand to bake in the sun until it's stiff as a board.

By following the simple steps just outlined, you'll return home with a catch in mint condition, ready for the final steps of scaling, cutting steaks, or filleting.

WHOLE FISH, FILLETS, AND STEAKS

Let's begin by taking your typical "round" fish, such as weakfish, striped bass, and bluefish. Many people prefer to cook these fish whole, and some even stuff the stomach cavity with a seasoned stuffing.

Use a fish scaler and work vigorously from the tail to the head of the fish. Because you've cared for the fish properly, the scales and skin will be moist, and the scales are easily removed. Don't apply too much pressure, which would bruise the delicate meat.

Many anglers then use scissors to cut away the dorsal, caudal, and anal fins, but this is a mistake, as it leaves the roots of the fins in the fish. When the fish is cooked the fin bones become those annoying bones that spoil a dinner. Instead, insert a sharp knife alongside the fins and cut from front to back, on both sides of the fin. Then grasp the dorsal and anal fins firmly and pull them out. In the case of the caudal fin, make a circular cut around the fin and pull it out as well.

You now have a whole fish, with scales and fins removed, ready for the chef to take over in the kitchen.

If, however, you prefer to steak the fish, particularly with large striped bass, all you have to do is cut away. Use a serrated knife, which makes a clean cut and easily cuts through the heavy backbone of large fish. Begin at the head, and cut off steaks of a desired thickness, working from front to back. As you get near the tail, the steaks become smaller, and many people just leave the section behind the anal fin whole.

A favorite method of cleaning fish is to fillet and skin them. The fillets lend themselves to almost any method of cooking and are especially easy to freeze, taking up little space in the freezer.

When you're filleting round fish, begin by inserting a sharp knife at the top of the head and cutting parallel to the dorsal fin, making the first cut from head to tail and deep enough so the knife cuts through the bones of the rib cage. As you pass the anal vent, there will be no more rib bones; the knife should be inserted so it exits the bottom of the fish, after which you continue cutting as tight to the backbone as possible until you reach the tail.

Make a cut at the head of the fish at an angle, so that as little meat as possible is wasted, cutting from top to bottom and working the knife just behind the caudal fin. If done properly you'll now have a slab from one side of the fish. Turn the fish over and repeat the same procedure.

Next, with the slab resting skin-side down, use your knife to carefully cut away the bones of the rib cage; again, take care not to waste any meat. You now have a true fillet, with no bones.

Next, remove the skin. Grasp the tail section of skin and work your knife back and forth toward the head, taking care not to cut through the skin. This is easily done when the fish is lying flat on a cutting board and the knife is sharp.

Perhaps the most important step of all is the next step. Round fish such as striped bass, bluefish, and weakfish have a lateral line that is very distinct and runs the length of the fish. Once you remove the skin you'll easily observe it as a piece of dark maroon-colored meat that runs the length of the fish. This meat has a strong flavor, and if you like your fish to have a mild taste, the lateral line is best removed.

To remove the lateral line, make a cut at a 45-degree angle from each side of the lateral line. When done properly you can then lift and

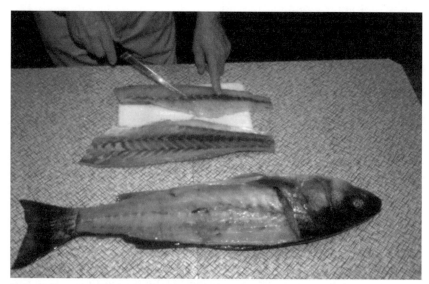

Striped bass, bluefish, and weakfish will have a milder flavor when filleted, the skin removed, and the dark meat of the lateral line removed.

remove the entire strip of dark-colored meat and discard it. You now have two fillets. With small fish the fillets are fine to cook whole. With larger fish, such as striped bass, many anglers cut thin fillets running the entire length of the fish.

FILLETING FLATFISH

Filleting "flat" fish such as fluke requires a somewhat different procedure. Begin by laying the flatfish on a cutting board before you. Insert the knife along the edge of the head, and cut until you feel the blade touching the backbone. Work the knife from the head to the tail, following the very distinct centerline on the flounder's back.

Use the knife to carefully cut from the center of the back, between the backbone and the meat, working the knife from the head to the tail, toward the fins. Finish by cutting the skin at the edge of the fins, working from head to tail, which results in a single fillet. Repeat the procedure, cutting another fillet from the top of the flounder. Now turn the flounder over, and repeat the same procedure on the white underside of the fish. You have four fillets.

Lay a fillet skin-side down, and work the knife from the tail of the fillet toward the head. You now have four fillets that represent the finest seafood you'll ever want to eat.

There are, of course, many variations on cleaning and caring for fish. As you become adept, you'll develop a style of your own. From my own observation, about 95 percent of the anglers who clean fish don't have a sharp knife—or a knife sharpener. Both are important tools. Often it's necessary to sharpen your knife several times while cleaning a big catch. Nice clean cuts are the result of a sharp knife. If you're hacking, pressing, and sawing, the knife is worthless, and you'll be wasting and bruising the fish in the bargain.

Freezing the Fish

When cleaned in a manner just described, the fish is ready for the kitchen, and there's just nothing better than freshly caught fish cooked immediately. Often, however, you may have more fish than you can use, and then freezing becomes an alternative. Here, too, most people put their cleaned fish in a plastic bag and place it in the freezer, after which it's all downhill; freezer burn takes over, and the fish begins to deteriorate.

For years it has been an accepted practice to freeze fish in a plastic bag filled with water; this resulted in the fish being frozen in a block of ice, where air and freezer burn couldn't harm it. This system works extremely well and is still an excellent way to freeze fish, except that the bulky packing takes up a lot of room in the freezer.

Today many anglers are vacuum packing their fish, using a neat Food Saver Vacuum Packaging System. It takes all of two minutes to learn how to use the Food Saver Vacuum Packer. It completely removes all air and results in a nice, neat package that takes practically no room in the freezer. Importantly, it extends the normal freezer life of frozen fish from six months to two years! If you catch and freeze your fish for the winter ahead, this is the way to go. When thawed, they taste as though you caught them that morning. A bonus is that you can use the system for vacuum packaging vegetables and meats as well.

By following the simple steps outlined in this chapter your catch will be in mint condition. The chef of the house can then take over. By using the recipes for striped bass, bluefish, weakfish, and fluke that June shares with you in the next chapter, you'll be treated to seafood dinners that qualify as a gourmet treat.

18

JUNE ROSKO'S RECIPES FOR THE BIG FOUR

There's no greater treat than returning home from a day along the seacoast and enjoying a delicious dinner of the fish you've caught earlier. Not only do anglers who fish for striped bass, weakfish, bluefish, and fluke enjoy a great contemplative pastime, but their catch constitutes some of the finest seafood the oceans have to offer.

Chapter 17 details the importance of properly handling the catch from the time it's landed until it reaches the kitchen. It cannot be overemphasized how important proper handling is to the quality of the fish reaching the cook.

At our house there's never a fishy smell when we're cooking fish. It's because the fish were handled properly and are being cooked properly. While there are thousands of seafood recipes using exotic herbs and spices and sauces, the recipes we're about to share here are plain and simple—and truly delicious. We challenge you to try them, and experience a whole new appreciation of the really fine taste of fresh seafood.

Baked Fish in Horseradish Sauce

It's always fun to try a new recipe for any fish. With few exceptions, the majority add a new dimension to the taste experience. Most recipes evolve, and this is such a recipe. It first appeared in an issue of *The Fisherman,* sent in by Greg Zaczek, an angler from Tuckerton, New Jersey. It included the following:

> 4 tablespoons mayonnaise
> 2 tablespoons mustard
> 1 tablespoon horseradish

4 fillets weighing about 1 pound
Grated Parmesan cheese to cover fillets

The recipe began by covering the bottom of a baking pan with oil or Pam cooking spray. Next the fillets were placed in the bottom of the pan.

The mayonnaise, mustard, and horseradish were mixed to make a smooth sauce. The sauce was then used to cover the fillets.

Finally, the sauce and fillets were covered with a light coating of Parmesan cheese.

Greg's recipe called for baking at 350 degrees for 20 minutes or until the top is golden.

Pete Barrett, the editor, tried the recipe and modified it somewhat. He baked the fillets for 10 minutes and then broiled them for 5 more minutes to get an extra-crispy coating from the cheese.

When we tried the recipe, using Pete's variation, we enjoyed it but found the horseradish somewhat overbearing. The second time we cut back on the horseradish, and there wasn't enough. The third time, and ever since, we've settled on a heaping teaspoon of horseradish as just the right amount. In our electric oven we found 6 or 7 minutes was sufficient, followed by 2 or 3 minutes in the broiler. In this way the fish didn't become dry.

After 50 years in the kitchen, here was a new recipe, with a touch of evolution provided by several people. It's a recipe you just must try with all four species, and any other fish you might care to try it with. Timing in the broiler should be just enough so the fish flakes easily at the touch of a fork and doesn't get dried out by overcooking.

Shortly thereafter we heard of another recipe that also capitalized on the use of horseradish, only with a different twist: sour cream. It's so simple it bears inclusion.

Broil any of the favorite four until they flake with a fork.

Separately, warm a cup of sour cream over very low heat, and add 1 teaspoon of horseradish—or adjust to taste—and stir it gently, making certain not to boil the sour cream. You want just enough heat to make it creamy. Then add a touch of salt, and cayenne if you wish.

When the fish comes out of the broiler, just spoon the sauce over the fish and garnish with sprigs of chive or chopped scallions. Delicious.

Greg recommended serving with a tossed salad with vinegar and oil.

We sliced some fresh Jersey tomatoes from the garden, added some steamed Jersey corn, and had a treat beyond words!

Fried Fish

While some may shudder at the thought of frying anything, when it comes to fresh fish, it's a method of cooking that few will dispute is "the best way to cook fish." Those watching their cholesterol level and calories can take heart in the recipe provided here. If you use Eggbeaters and canola oil it solves some of the concern, and the fish taste excellent.

> 4 fillets of the favorite four cut to size,
>   measuring 1/2 by 2 by 8 inches
> 1 package Eggbeaters (equivalent of 2 whole eggs)
> 1 cup seasoned bread crumbs
> 1 cup enriched flour
> 1/2 cup canola oil

The flour in this recipe helps make the coating thicker than bread crumbs alone. It can be eliminated if you prefer just bread crumbs.

Dredge the moist fillets in the flour, so they're completely white.

Dip the fillets in Eggbeaters. When thoroughly coated, place the fillets in the seasoned bread crumbs and thoroughly coat. You'll find that the Eggbeaters have a somewhat pasty consistency, sticking to the fillets more readily than whole eggs. This makes for a tasty, crunchy crust that adheres nicely to the fillet.

The most important consideration in frying the favorite four is to begin with an 8- or 10-inch frying pan filled approximately 1/4 inch deep with canola oil, and heated until it's piping hot over medium heat. Avoid placing the fillets in cold oil. When you place the fillets in the frying pan it should be sizzling hot, and immediately begin to fry. Check the fillets after a few minutes, lifting a corner with a fork. When they take on a dark golden color you know they're ready to turn. Take extra care when frying the second side, for it will fry faster than the first side. You know they're done when the delicate meat flakes at the touch of a fork. Remove the fillets from the frying pan and place them on paper toweling, which will absorb excess oil. Take care not to fry them too long, as this tends to dry out the fish; they take on a chewy consistency.

As with most fish recipes, serve with freshly picked tomatoes, corn on the cob, or garden vegetables for a gourmet treat that can't be beat.

Fish Cakes

Striped bass and fluke have a heavier texture than bluefish and weakfish, but all may be used in a change-of-pace fish cake recipe that's easy to prepare and absolutely delicious.

This recipe came to us from Al Wutkowski, one of the most renowned striped bass anglers on the Atlantic coast. Al spent a lot of time experimenting and eventually wound up with a recipe that's difficult to beat.

> 2 pounds fillets, preferably striped bass
> 1 cup chopped Vidalia onions
> 1 cup chopped green or red bell peppers
> 1 cup whole-kernel corn
> 2 tablespoons virgin olive oil
> 2 tablespoons mayonnaise
> 1 tablespoon Dijon mustard
> 1 package Eggbeaters (equivalent of 2 whole eggs)
> Old Bay Seasoning and hot red pepper flakes to taste
> 2 cups seasoned bread crumbs
> Canola oil for frying

Cut the fillets into 3- or 4-inch cubes. Then steam or poach them for 8 to 10 minutes, or until the meat flakes at the touch of a fork. Drain the fillet cubes in a colander, pressing out as much water as you can, so the delicate meat is nearly dry.

In a small frying pan, sauté the olive oil, onions, peppers, and corn until the onions have caramelized—turning a rich golden color—and the vegetables are tender. Remove the pan from the heat and set aside for later use.

In a large mixing bowl, mix the mayonnaise, mustard, Eggbeaters, and sautéed vegetables. If you like your fish cakes spicy, now's the time to add Old Bay Seasoning and red pepper flakes, to suit your taste.

Finally, add the fish and mix with your hands until the fish flakes into small pieces the size of crabmeat chunks. Add the seasoned bread crumbs, just enough to hold the mixture together, making it easy to form into fish cakes.

You can make fish cakes of uniform size by using a 1/4- or 1/3-cup plastic measuring cup, and packing the mixture tightly into the cup. Hold the cup's handle and slap it hard, facedown, into the palm of your hand. This will pop the mixture out of the cup in a nicely formed fish cake of perfect size.

Place the canola oil in a frying pan and make certain it's sizzling hot before you put the fish cakes in. Fry the fish cakes in canola oil, using just enough oil so they're not covered. Fry the fish cakes until they're a golden brown. Always remember it takes less time to fry the second side after you turn them over.

If you prefer not to fry, place the fish cakes on a cookie sheet sprayed with Pam cooking spray, and bake them in an oven at 350 degrees. They usually require approximately 30 minutes to bake, or until they take on a golden brown color.

When the fish cakes are removed from the frying pan or oven, place them on paper toweling and permit them to drain and cool. They take on a more delicate flavor after just 5 minutes of cooling. They're delicious when served with tartar sauce or a hot horseradish cocktail sauce.

Should you make more fish cakes than you can use at one sitting, freeze them with a vacuum packer for later use.

Fish Chowder

Simple is usually better, and this fish chowder recipe is just that. It can be made with ingredients that are readily available, and is absolutely delicious. Importantly, it's a basic recipe that isn't overpowering, and you can adjust it to suit your taste as you go along.

> 2 large Vidalia onions, chopped
> 1/4 cup margarine
> 1 1/2 quarts water
> 12 tiny carrots, peeled and cut
>   in 1/4-inch pieces

5 medium-sized red potatoes,
   peeled and cut in 1/2-inch cubes
1 1/2 pounds striped bass or fluke fillets
2 cups 1 percent milk
1 12-ounce can evaporated milk

Sauté the chopped onions in the margarine in a large soup pot until they're caramelized and take on a rich golden color. Add the water, carrots, and potatoes and set on the range at simmer. When the carrots and potatoes are tender to the fork, add the fish fillets and continue to simmer. When the fish begins to flake, add the 2 cups of milk and 1 can of evaporated milk. Add salt and pepper, Old Bay Seasoning, or cayenne pepper to suit your taste. You can even add bell peppers or whole-kernel corn to the recipe if you wish, both of which add flavor.

With all of the ingredients now combined, continue stirring lightly on simmer until it's hot, but do not boil the fish chowder.

A generous portion of old-fashioned Oysterettes added to the chowder makes it just great. You'll find a large bowl of this fish chowder perfect with a sandwich for lunch, or as a great beginning to dinner.

Steamed Fish

For many years chefs used either a poacher or steam rack to steam their fish. Today's chefs most often employ a piece of heavy-duty aluminum foil, wrapping their fish in the foil and steaming it in the oven or on the grill. This results in a steamed fish that has just the right texture. The flavor is enhanced as it's being steamed.

It's the perfect way to make a delicious dinner from any of the favorite four, and there's no mess to clean up afterward.

Sufficient 1/2-inch-thick fillets for each portion
Mayonnaise to coat
4 slices Vidalia onion per portion
4 slices tomato per portion
Thinly sliced bell peppers and mushrooms
   per portion
Salt and pepper to taste
12-inch by 12-inch piece of aluminum foil per portion

Begin by setting your oven at 350 degrees, or lighting your outdoor grill, so it's sufficiently hot by the time you prepare the portion-sized packets.

Place a portion-sized fillet or two at the center of the aluminum foil. Coat each fillet with approximately 1/8 inch of mayonnaise. Place 4 slices of Vidalia onion and 4 slices of tomato on top of each fillet. Add the thinly sliced bell peppers and mushrooms, spreading them evenly over the tomatoes. Lightly salt and pepper to taste.

Join the aluminum foil together atop the fillets and vegetables, and fold it over twice, drawing your finger across the foil to make a tight seal. Now fold each end over twice, making a tight seal.

Place the aluminum packets of fish and vegetable directly onto the grill, or onto a cookie sheet if you're steaming them in the oven. If the oven or grill is hot, you can expect the fish and vegetables to be steamed and tender in 8 to 10 minutes. You can test a packet by carefully opening it, avoiding the steam that is quickly released, and ensuring that the fillets flake easily, indicating they're done.

Open each packet and place it right onto the dinner plate, discarding the foil. No pots, pans, or cleanup needed!

Served with a garden salad, this is a great seafood recipe, ideal for summer entertaining on the deck, for you can make up the packets beforehand and just pop them onto the grill for a quick, delicious dinner of steamed fish and veggies.

Stuffed Fish

Stuffing chicken, duck, veal, and pork is a ritual at many households, yet it's surprising how few people stuff fish. Little do they realize they're missing a seafood delight.

Stripers, weakfish, blues, and fluke can be stuffed whole. The fillets may be formed into portions, either one atop another, or formed into doughnut shapes held together with toothpicks. The stuffing is placed into the stomach cavity, a pocket in the fillets, or the doughnut hole, as the case may be.

> 8 small fluke fillets or a 5- or 6-pound bluefish,
> weakfish, or striper

1 green bell pepper
1 red bell pepper
6 small white button mushrooms
1 large Vidalia onion
2 tablespoons margarine
Salt and pepper to taste
1 cup seasoned bread crumbs

Before you begin preparing the ingredients, set the oven at 350 degrees. You always want your oven piping hot before the fish goes in, as it then begins to cook immediately and prevents the fish from drying out.

Dice the peppers, mushrooms, and onion into small pieces, about 1/4 inch square. Place the vegetables in a saucepan and add the margarine. Sauté over medium heat until the onions are caramelized and take on a golden color and the vegetables are done.

Juices will build up in the pan during the sautéing, and when you add the seasoned bread crumbs and salt and pepper, they'll all cling together in a pastelike consistency. Sample a spoonful to make certain it's seasoned to suit your taste buds, and if necessary, adjust accordingly.

When stuffing whole fish, open the stomach cavity and, using a spoon, fill it until it bulges, ensuring a good quantity of stuffing in each fish. With fillets formed into doughnuts and held together with toothpicks, fill the hole in the doughnut to the top. If the fillets are placed one atop the other, spread the stuffing between the fillets; if they're thick fillets, slice a pocket in the fillet and fill it. In each case, place a dab of margarine on the fillets, or several pieces of margarine on a whole fish, to keep it moist while baking.

Place the stuffed fish on a cookie sheet sprayed with Pam cooking spray and pop it into the hot oven. Next, make certain to set the timer so you don't overcook it. Remember, the stuffing is still hot and has been cooked, so all you've got to worry about is baking the fish. In most cases the fish will be done in 8 minutes, but check thin fillets after 6 minutes, and remove them as soon as they flake at the touch of a fork. With larger, whole fish weighing several pounds, you have to check regularly until the meat flakes and lifts away from the backbone, which will take longer than the fillets.

For those of you who are innovators, dicing sea scallops or including chunks of crabmeat in the stuffing will add to its already great flavor.

Blackened Fish

Blackened redfish took the country by storm a few years back. It brought innovators to the kitchen, too, who quickly found other fish that could replace the threatened redfish population. Striped bass had the same texture, and for coastal anglers immediately became the fish of choice.

It was Chef Paul Prudhomme whose Blackened Redfish Magic in a shaker jar not only popularized the recipe, but also made purchasing and using the seasoning popular. There was only one catch—the smoke problem. Blacken striped bass in your kitchen and you'll fill the room with dense smoke, no matter how good your exhaust fan. Best bet is to do it outdoors on the grill.

> Striped bass steaks cut to 1 inch thick
> 1 shaker jar Chef Paul Prudhomme's Blackened
>   Redfish Magic seasoning
> Pam cooking spray

Place a cast-iron skillet on the grill 10 minutes before you plan to cook, so it gets sizzling hot.

Spray both sides of the striper steaks with Pam cooking spray. Apply a liberal coating of Chef Paul's blackened fish seasoning to both sides.

Carefully place the steaks in the skillet, for they'll immediately begin to sizzle, and the smoke will be intense. Cook the underside until the blackening forms a tasty crust. After you turn it over, watch the fish closely; the second side cooks faster than the first. Test regularly with a fork, and as soon as the fish flakes, it's done. Don't overcook it!

Be extra careful when handling the skillet. Always use a pot holder or heat-resistant glove, as it gets extremely hot and can cause severe burns if you're careless.

Blackened striped bass is delicious unto itself. Add a nice salad and fresh steamed zucchini, eggplant, mushrooms, peppers, and onions and you've a treat that's difficult to beat.

Battered Fish

Pieces of the favorite four coated with a heavy batter and deep-fried are an exciting change of pace at the dinner table. The fish's flavor is captured within the batter and the bite-sized pieces or fingers are light and crunchy.

THE BATTER: 1 package Eggbeaters (equivalent of 2 whole eggs)
1/2 teaspoon granulated sugar
4 heaping tablespoons flour
8 dashes Worcestershire sauce
Salt and pepper to taste
Sufficient skim milk to give a heavy consistency
    to the batter

It takes a few extra minutes to batter and fry small pieces, but bite-sized pieces are the key to enjoying this recipe, so cut small and enjoy!

Mix all of the batter ingredients together and use an electric mixer to beat until the batter takes on a creamy consistency.

Place the batter mixture in the refrigerator for a couple of hours to set, and remove it about half an hour before you plan to use it.

Be liberal with the canola oil in the frying pan, of sufficient depth to cover the small pieces. Keep the frying pan and oil over moderate heat while you're battering the fish, so it's hot when you drop the battered fish into it.

Begin by lightly salting and peppering the fingers, then dip them in the creamy batter, so they're thoroughly covered.

Drop the fingers into the oil and they'll immediately begin sizzling, securing the fish's flavor and juices within the batter. It'll take only a couple of minutes on each side for them to take on a rich, golden brown color. With battered fish you can sometimes fry them a little longer than with other methods, particularly if you like a dark, crunchy crust.

Place the battered fingers on paper toweling as you remove them from the frying pan. Then sit back and enjoy!

Smoked Fish

So often it's said that plain and simple is best. Such is the case when smoking fish. All too often exotic recipes are brought into play, with special brines that diminish the fine flavor of fish, and combinations of wood and excessive smoking time reducing the fish to dry and tasteless.

The recipe included here will result in the finest-tasting smoked striped bass, weakfish, bluefish, and fluke you've ever eaten. You can use it for trout and catfish, too—almost any fish that swims, for that matter.

You'll require a Little Chef Electric Smoker or a comparable, easy-to-use smoker. To smoke three 12-inch by 12-inch wire racks of either whole small fish or fillets you'll need the following ingredients:

> 1 package hickory- or apple-wood smoking chips
> 1/2 cup noniodized salt
> 1/2 cup white granulated sugar
> 1 quart tap water

Begin by making a brine solution, mixing the noniodized salt and granulated sugar and adding it to 1/2 quart of warm tap water. Place the cap on the jar and shake it vigorously until the salt and sugar are dissolved. Then fill the quart jar to the top with cold water and shake again vigorously.

Chill the brine and place it in a Pyrex or glass baking dish. Do not use a metal dish or pan.

Next, place the fillets or whole fish you plan to smoke in the brine. Leave the skin on the fillets, as this holds the smoked fish together. If the whole fish are too big for the smoker's racks, cut them into pieces that will fit. You can remove the head and tail if necessary, but leave the skin on, as this holds in the juices and prevents the fish from becoming dry.

The brine time varies from fish to fish. Small fish or fillets may only require 8 hours in brine, while thicker chunks require 12 hours. An easy practice is to place them in the refrigerator, turning them at least once, so the fish is thoroughly brined. The brine time is a matter of personal taste. Too little may not have the tang you want in your smoked fish, while too long often takes on a salty taste.

The final step before smoking is to remove the fish from the brine and wash each piece in cold water. Pat the pieces dry with paper toweling, and permit them to dry in the air for at least an hour. You'll notice that the fish will take on a tacky glaze, called the pellicle.

Place the smoker outside, preferably in an airy yet protected spot, where the smoke won't be offensive. Turn the smoker on while the fish is air-drying, so that it's hot before you place the fish in it. Do not add the wood smoking chips.

Spray the smoker's grills with Pam cooking spray, as this makes it easier washing them afterward, which can be done in your dishwasher.

Once the pellicle is present on the fish to be smoked, place the fish and pieces on the smoker's grills and insert them in place on the upright rack, which is inserted into the smoker.

All of the favorite four are delicious when smoked. You'll need an electric smoker, hickory- or apple-wood smoking chips, and either small whole fish, chunks of fish, or fillets. It's a smoked-fish treat that can't be beat.

Now fill the smoker's pan with wood chips and insert it into the smoker. The heating element of the smoker will quickly cause the wood chips to begin smoldering, giving off smoke, which will rise upward in the smoker, surround the fish, and exit from the top.

It usually requires half an hour or so for the wood chips to smolder to the point that they're totally black and no longer emit smoke. Remove the pan of chips and refill it, which will require another hour of smoking. When the second pan of chips has turned black, the smoking process is complete. While the fish is smoked, however, it's not yet sufficiently dry to remove from the smoker.

It will require an additional 6, 8, or even 10 hours of drying time for the heat of the smoker to dry the fish. Taste a small piece periodically once it begins to take on a golden color. Remove when it achieves the desired texture. Here it's extremely important that the fish be moist and tasty, not dry and chewy. Your taste buds will tell you when it's time to remove it from the smoker.

Smoked fish should be refrigerated in an odorproof container; otherwise everything will take on a smoked smell. It'll keep for up to 10 days or so, but should be frozen if you plan on keeping it longer. It's really best to smoke a small amount of the favorite four as you need them, so the flavor and texture will be perfect.

As a snack at cocktail time, or a luncheon treat, smoked fish are just a delight. Only by smoking them at home will you gain appreciation of this unique way of preparing fish fresh from the sea.

Caramelized Roasted Vegetables

Fish and salads are a natural, and usually the produce department at your supermarket has a fine selection of greens and salad fixings to prepare a crisp beginning to a seafood dinner.

With vegetables it's something else again, and people often tire of vegetables prepared with conventional recipes. A super recipe that you're sure to enjoy with almost any of the recipes presented here is to caramelize vegetables in a roasting pan or Pyrex dish. It's easy to make, and you can use your imagination and practically any and all the veggies you like.

1 small eggplant
1 small zucchini or yellow squash
1 large green pepper
1 large red pepper
2 large Vidalia onions
6 medium white mushrooms
6 large tomatoes
1–4 crushed garlic cloves
2 tablespoons virgin olive oil
Salt and pepper to taste
1 handful fresh basil or 1 tablespoon dry basil

Peel the eggplant, squash, and peppers and cut into 1/2-inch squares. Cut the remaining vegetables into 1/2-inch squares.

Place the vegetables into a roasting pan or Pyrex baking dish and sprinkle the virgin olive oil over them, along with salt and pepper to taste. Sprinkle the basil over the vegetables and mix the ingredients together. You'll be stirring often, so make certain to use the longest-handled spoon you have.

Set the oven at 525 degrees and let it heat for 10 minutes, so it's hot when you put the vegetables in.

Often the pan will be filled to overflowing, but it will quickly cook down and should be stirred at 5-minute intervals; with the intense heat, the vegetables on the bottom will burn if they're not turned. It takes about half an hour for the vegetables to cook down, and there'll be quite a bit of juice accumulating.

Taste the vegetables; when they're tender, change the oven setting from baking to broiling and leave the oven door open. Continue stirring for 5 or 10 more minutes, until the vegetables turn a rich, golden brown color, indicating they've caramelized, thickening as the liquid slowly disappears. As this happens you may feel you want a richer color, and with the liquid almost gone, it may be necessary to add a little water and continue to let it cook down, until it reaches the desired color, flavor, and consistency.

The recipes included here are our favorites for the favorite four. There are no doubt many more recipes for these fine fish. Use these as a beginning. You may like them as we do, or you may wish to be innovative, adding more seasoning, a bit of cayenne, or whatever suits your taste. You can serve with horseradish cocktail sauce, melted butter, tartar sauce, or just plain ketchup. Whatever suits your taste is what's important. Don't be afraid to be innovative in the kitchen. It makes for more enjoyment after a fun-filled day along the seacoast catching the favorite four.

End of a perfect day.

CONCLUSION

The conclusion of a book usually represents the end. For the readers who have arrived at this point, however, it's hopefully the beginning of an exciting new adventure. For newcomers, I hope you've gained the knowledge that will enable you to move forth and employ the fundamentals that will enhance your enjoyment. For veteran anglers it's a foregone conclusion you'll be right out there trying every tip you've gleaned from these pages. Perhaps it's trying a Clouser teaser, maybe the breeches buoy rig. Whatever, if you find just one tip successful, this book will have been worthwhile.

Almost every author likes to write light, easy reading, where the reader is swept up in the story. Writing personal adventure yarns about stripers, fluke, weakfish, and blues would have been fun to write, and fun to read. Remembering all those fond memories of a lifetime on the water is what fishing for the favorite four is all about. Swapping fish tales with fellow anglers is almost as much fun as the actual experience.

Unfortunately, or perhaps fortunately, this book took the conservative route, attempting to cram between the covers as much information as possible that you can put to use along the seacoast. Absorb and use all the techniques, and by all means try June's recipes. If you do, the book will have served its purpose, for which the authors will be eternally pleased.